MAVERICKS

nine independent publishers

Compiled by

RICHARD PEABODY

PAYCOCK PRESS

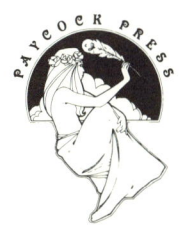

Acknowledgements:

"George Braziller (of George Braziller) Talks About . . . " was reprinted from the January 15, 1982 issue of *Publishers Weekly*, published by R.R. Bowker Company, a Xerox Company, Copyright © 1982 by Xerox Corporation.

The Maurice Girodias Interview was reprinted from *Gargoyle* 22/23, © Spring 1983.

"An Interview with David Godine" was reprinted from *GRANTA* no. 4, © 1981.

"James Laughlin of New Directions" © 1981 by The New York Times Company. Reprinted by Permission.

"A Happy Publisher" © 1980 by The New York Times Company. Reprinted by Permission.

"An Influence on the Language: An Interview with James Boyer May" reprinted from *Southern California Lit Scene* vol. 1, no. 2, © Jan. 1971 and vol. 1, no. 3, © Feb.-June 1971.

"Barney Rosset, the Force Behind Grove Press" was reprinted from the *Washington Star* © August 12, 1979.

"Alan Swallow" was reprinted from *Publishing in the West: Alan Swallow*, edited by William F. Claire, and published by The Lightning Tree Press, Santa Fe, New Mexico, © 1974.

"Capra: SB's Big Little Press" was reprinted from the *Santa Barbara News & Review* © December 15, 1977.

Paycock logo by Roy Comiskey
Printed in the U.S.A.
ISBN: 0-9602424-9-X
Library of Congress No. 82-61464

Copyright © 1983 by Richard Myers Peabody, Jr.
All rights revert to the individual authors
or copyright owners.

The Paycock Press
P.O. Box 3567
Washington, D.C. 20007

Mavericks

Dedicated to all small publishers who labor in obscurity and for John and Marian Pomeroy who believed in me from the very beginning.

Contents

George Braziller   11
Maurice Girodias   27
David Godine   40
James Laughlin   55
John Martin   65
James Boyer May   73
Barney Rosset   103
Alan Swallow   117
Noel Young   123

Preface

This book reprints interviews with, or profiles of, nine independent publishers. In no way have I attempted to gather pieces on *every* publisher, and I have of course left out many. I think what I was really after, in selecting these publishers and their presses, was a book I could hand to those who ask *why* I do what I do. The resulting volume is a nine-part answer, a rationale.

—Richard Peabody

George Braziller

GEORGE BRAZILLER : *New York*

George Braziller (of George Braziller) Talks About...

Twenty-six years after its founding, George Braziller, Inc., remains in its originator's hands. A long career in the book business, dating back to the founding of an influential book club in 1942, has dulled not a whit of the publisher's commitment to good books. Long before the elevators at One Park Avenue have begun disgorging other executives, the 65-year-old Braziller can be found already at his desk. He arrives at work most days by 8:15, and except during inclement weather, walks from home to his office—some 40-odd blocks.

Once referred to as "the most independent of the independent publishers," the low-key Braziller hardly lives up to that description on first acquaintance. He is unfailingly courteous to visitors, who inevitably leave with books in hand. "Independence," in Braziller's lexicon, means total control over the publishing operation. More perhaps than any contemporary publisher, George Braziller personifies the house he built.

Before hanging out his publishing shingle in 1955, Braziller had already made a name for himself as creator of the Book Find Club, a venture that only three years after its founding attracted 70,000 members and notice from *Time* magazine. Both the Book Find Club and a sister club, the Seven Arts Book Society, were sold to Time Inc. in 1969. Braziller's share of the sale—$350,000—was used to finance the publishing house. He now owns 51% of George Braziller, Inc., with the remaining interest shared by sons Michael, founder and president of Persea Books, and Joel, an attorney.

As a book publisher, Braziller is best known for its art and architecture titles and for literature from abroad. The first volume of its illuminated manuscript series—*The Hours of Catherine of Cleves*—won the 1966 Carey-Thomas Award, sponsored by *Publishers Weekly*. The house received the distinction of a second Carey-Thomas in 1979, for its "exceptional publishing program embracing art books and innovative fiction from the U.S. and abroad." Braziller is the only publisher to have received the award twice and also the only one to have been cited for an entire publishing program. Authors who at one time or another have been published by Braziller include Langston Hughes, Sean O'Casey, Vincent Scully, Jr., Josiah Bunting, Pavel Kohout, Daniel and Elizabeth Moynihan, Octavio Paz, Janet Frame, Ned Rorem, Ronald Glasser and Beryl Bainbridge. Many have remained on its list. The two chief luminaries in nonfiction are art historian and professor emeritus Meyer Schapiro (*Modern Art: 19th and 20th Centuries*) and historian Emmanuel LeRoy Ladurie (*Montaillou*). In 1970, Braziller inaugurated the Braziller Poetry Series, which now includes over 20 volumes from contemporary poets, Cynthia MacDonald, Charles Simic and Norman Rosten among them.

Given his achievements, Braziller's position within the publishing industry is curious. More accurately, his position is *outside* it. Rarely does he see American agents (or, as he says, rarely do they come to him), and he has little contact with such trade associations as the Association of American Publishers (which, coincidentally, is his neighbor at One Park Avenue).

The conversation that follows, with *PW*'s Stella Dong, was spread out over several visits in the late fall of 1981.

Interviewer: The writers you published at the start of your career were Europeans—Jean-Paul Sartre and the French nouveau roman writers like Nathalie Sarraute, Claude Simon and Claude Mauriac. Then you moved on to Italian, German, English and even Nigerian wirters. Now it's the new generation of Irish and Australian writers you're publishing—Desmond Hogan, Neil Jordan, Niall Quinn, Bernard MacLaverty, David Malouf, Kate Cruise O'Brien and David Ireland. The American authors are few. Why the heavy emphasis on writers from abroad?

Braziller: It's a combination of many things. In 1955, when I started out, I knew I wanted to do fiction. But I wasn't about to go around to all the name authors in the States to see what they were doing. And if I sat back, waiting for the manuscripts to come in, I wouldn't be publishing anything. I knew something was happening in Paris at that time, and I was looking for good writers, so I went straight to Paris. At the time, there was a totally different attitude there towards myself as a publisher. The publishers and agents in Europe treated me as if I were any other American publisher. They were sympathetic, receptive and grateful—and that's what kept me going. So, it was not that I thought the French writers were better than the Americans, or later, the English better than the French. Not at all. When Gunter Grass writes from Germany, he knows he's writing for a world audience, and it's world criticism he's concerned about. It was the same for me. My movements weren't up and down Madison Avenue. They were across boundaries and borders.

Interviewer: What was your attitude toward American literary agents—or rather, what were their dealings with you? And has it changed much?

Braziller: I doubt that more than 2% of any list I've ever published consists of agented material. At the time I started, agents simply weren't submitting anything to us, and if they were submitting certain writers, they just weren't good enough. Agents in America, if they have a good writer, naturally will think of the more established publishing house over our house. I don't blame them for that. Agents know damn well that all they're interested in is getting as much money for their authors as they possibly can. Maybe they'll pretend to say this is the right publisher for this author—but that's nonsense. I know the game.

Interviewer: You've had the frequent experience of developing writers—and Americans at that—who have subsequently gone on to a larger house once they've become successful. Can you do anything to counteract that situation?

Braziller: No, it is a fact of the business, and I don't fault any authors for it. It's fairly well known that I published the first novel of a Korean writer [*The Martyred* by Richard Kim] to great success, and then another publisher and the author's agent came up with a $50,000 advance for the second book. This has happened with a number of other writers we have put on our list. I don't blame them. There's no point, from our point of view, in keeping on an author who's unhappy and wants to leave. The only reason we've been able to keep Beryl Bainbridge, for instance, is that she has insisted that she remain with me. We know for a fact that recently Beryl was offered $50,000 by two or three American publishers, and chose not to leave.

Interviewer: Would Beryl Bainbridge be your most successful author in terms of number of books sold?

Braziller: Yes . . . but I'm a little embarrassed to give you the numbers because they're probably not what you think they are. Actually Jean-Paul Sartre's *The Words* might be the biggest selling book on our list. That sold about 35,000 copies. As you can tell, we just don't publish bestsellers. I'm not even sure if we've ever made a bestseller list—maybe once, with *The Words*, perhaps.

Interviewer: Aside from your literary publishing, George Braziller, Inc., is well known for its extensive art and architecture backlist. What percentage of your total backlist consists of books in the art and architecture category, and what are some of your more popular series or titles?

Braziller: Our art and architecture books must account for about 80% of our inventory. We did a series called the Great Ages of World Architecture. Then came the American Artists series, which was followed by the medieval art program, which we started in 1966. We now have 15 of the facsimiles in print. And if you want to talk about bestsellers, a book like *The Tres Riches Heures of Jean, Duke of Berry* has sold, all over the world, over 100,000 copies. *The Hours of Catherine of Cleves* has sold over 100,000 copies. The architecture series sells year after year. And the backlist now seems far more impressive than if you sell, say 30,000 or 40,000 copies of a novel the first year and then it stops dead.

Interviewer: To what degree do you rely on co-publishing agreements with foreign publishers to support your art book publishing, which must undoubtedly be a costly undertaking? What role does the relatively higher cost of the art and architecture titles play in the stability of the house?

Braziller: Though we have published series, like the American Artists or the architecture series, that do not involve co-editions, virtually all of our art books—the ones we ourselves originate—require foreign co-publication. This has been the key to the success or to the continuance of the house. The nature of art book publishing is such that you need large editions. It's an expensive proposition and you need as much help as you can get. So you go to England, France, Germany, Italy and so on to convince them or sell them some of your ideas, or the books themselves. It's true that these books are very important to our backlist, simply because of the billing that they generate. Some of them, especially the architecture titles, are used in many courses. We have a tremendous investment in the books in that category, and though they're expensive, I like to believe they're worthwhile books.

Interviewer: Have you altered your accounting and warehousing practices in order to comply with the *Thor* ruling? Considering the relatively higher value of your titles, were you hit particularly hard by *Thor*?

Braziller: Yes, I was, and perhaps it was our own fault for ignorance of the law. I'm not going to say whether the law was right or wrong, or just or unjust. But it hurt us. We are now analyzing our inventory, and unfortunately we are destroying sheets. We no longer can keep certain titles in print, much as we would like to. I don't want to take the position that the government should be blamed for this decision. I don't feel book publishers should be treated any differently from plumbers or other manufacturers. Many people argue that books are different from pliers or hammers. Well, sometimes I think a good hammer is better than a bad book. It's incumbent on us as publishers to run our businesses carefully and not look to blame anyone else. It's easy to blame the IRS, or the booksellers, or bad reviews. I don't think, now that I'm functioning again after the *Thor* decision, that I'm any better or worse for it, and I don't think authors are going to be any the better or worse either.

Interviewer: In 1942 you started the Book Find Club, a national book club competing with the two majors—the Book-of-the-Month Club and the Literary Guild. Less than 10 years later, membership reached the high mark of 100,000. Is it possible to operate a book club based on a similar philosophy, offering books of distinction at low prices, today?

Braziller: It would be difficult. There are now maybe 30 or 40 specialty book clubs in existence, which was not so when I started the Book Find Club. Also, virtually all of the book clubs offer alternates, something they didn't do in the early years of the Book-of-the-

Month Club or the Literary Guild. By only offering a single book each, you can see many were being overlooked, and that's where the Book Find Club came in. Now the major clubs take maybe a half dozen or a dozen alternates in a single month. And the biggest factor is the quality paperbacks. There isn't a single major work of literature that can't be obtained in paperback today. And there is also the Quality Paperback Book Club, so you see, I certainly couldn't dream of starting another Book Find Club today.

Interviewer: In running the Book Find Club, you built up quite a substantial mailing list and perhaps even developed some sophisticated direct-mail marketing techniques. Were you able to apply your knowledge of direct marketing to the publishing business?

Braziller: Well, that was the biggest mistake I ever made. With all my experience and knowledge of mail order in running the Book Find Club and Seven Arts, I just wanted to get away from it and go into the publishing business. Actually, I find mail order one of the most skillful, interesting methods of marketing or selling that exists, because it is a science. It's so much fun. I don't know why I shied away from it all these years. What I should have done was to proceed with developing a mailing list and mail order business, because ultimately, that is what's going to save the small independent publisher. At a recent dinner party sponsored by B. Dalton, I listened to the company's plans for the next three to five years, and while I'd like to feel that somehow a small publisher can fit into that program, I have some doubts about it. One thing I do not have doubts about is that unless we develop our own means of marketing, small publishers like ourselves will not survive. First and foremost, that means mail order.

Interviewer: But how can a trade publisher succeed by using that strategy if the list appeals to a large and general audience?

Braziller: It's expensive and risky, but it can be done. Now this might mean specialization, and that frightens me. I don't like to feel that I'm being categorized as a publisher of only architecture books or of Irish literature or anything. Fiction is particularly hard to sell through mail order. When I say mail order, this is not an either/or proposition. There's room for every area. I don't imply that we're going to give up reaching the customer through the bookstore—every area has to be looked at. But we don't do it enough. There are endless methods of selling books, whether it's giveaways, or premiums, or mail orders to bookstores, or the book clubs, or reprint houses, or whatever. I suppose it depends on whether one can afford to explore all these marketing areas. We know we have a following around the country of about 3000-5000 hardcore customers who want every illuminated manuscript that we publish. If we had made the effort and kept the names and developed the names, I believe we would have had a list now of about 20,000-25,000 people. Just this morning, I got a request from a little society called the Ephemera Society. I never heard of them. But they have 1000 members and they're interested in a book that we publish—*200 Years of American Graphic Art*. Now a good marketing person in a publishing house should have known about that. But we don't function that way. We publish and then hope to find a market.

Interviewer: What's your split of retail versus mail order sales, and what categories have you most successfully marketed by direct mail?

Braziller: The ratio is 95% retail to 5% mail order. Bookstore sales are roughly 50 or 60%, with the remainder being the institutional market. Without question, our art and architecture titles are most successfully sold through direct mail. These sales are to schools, libraries, and adoptions—also to people just writing in.

Interviewer: You talked a bit about how you don't see a place for publishers like yourself in the future scheme of a chain like B. Dalton. Independent booksellers say the chains are eating them up, that the chains and discounters will drive them out of business, and that the market for good books will disappear. What do you think?

Braziller: The problems are real. When I published quality fiction, 10 years ago, for an interesting new writer it was with a 2000-3000-copy sales advance, and this went to 800-1000 bookstores. It sold in twos, threes, and fours. When it came to returns, we'd get back maybe 10%-15%. The books were ordered by a thousand individual, independent little bookstores who cared when we walked in and showed them one of our new authors. They'd more or less find a customer for those twos, threes and fours. These days I plan an 800-copy printing for quality fiction. What I'm faced with as the current alternative is to go to the chains with a first author, and they want to know: *a)* how much we're printing, and *b)* how much we're spending on advertising, before they'll make a commitment. If we're not printing 10,000 or 15,000 copies and we're not going to spend

$15,000 to 20,000 on advertising, they won't order the book.

Interviewer: As you say, your house has never been famous for its bestsellers. Looking over your list, it seems fair to say that you've never brought out a title that didn't reflect your own taste, or one that you didn't think deserved to reach an intelligent audience. In other words, you have never published a book specifically for its commercial value. If you had, wouldn't you be better off financially?

Braziller: There's no question that money, capital, is important to running not only a publishing house, but any business. But money alone is not the answer. We know, for example, that there are very few publishing houses that have more money than McGraw-Hill. And McGraw-Hill has made a dismal failure in trade publishing over the last 30-40 years. I'm always amused by editors who go from one house to another, and they are told the same things—that they will have the company's complete support, that money will always be available to them, and so on. No, I'm afraid it's more than money. Money is an important thing, but you also need other factors, like talent and luck and making the best use of your resources.

Interviewer: You've never cared to hire one of these high-priced editors?

Braziller: No; and one of the reasons for that is that high-priced editors and what goes with them is something that we could not afford. Any big editor feels he or she should have money to commission books or to get authors and give them big advances. We never operated that way. And in addition, take the big editors in the trade—particularly those in their 40s or 50s right now. That is an interesting group. I don't care to name names, but all of these editors are really extremely talented and have good taste. But because of the salaries that they command—of necessity—they have to work on the big commercial books. Any editor making $100,000 a year cannot afford to work on a quality work of fiction. It's usually assigned to some associate editor or some editor they want to keep interested. It's a dichotomy in a way that I find ironic—that the most qualified editors in publishing are working on books that they're not particularly happy about. They all admit that they buy the big commercial books, and that's where they're spending most of their time, whether they like it or not.

Braziller 21

Interviewer: Still, wouldn't the additional funds generated by a few bestseller sales contribute greatly to your ability to better promote the books you believe in? You've mentioned that you have authors whose books you would love to add to your spring list, but you don't feel that it's possible at the moment. Again, wouldn't the more profitable books somewhat alleviate that problem?

Braziller: There is an author—A.L. Barker, an Englishwoman whose books have won considerable praise here and in England. I published her most recent book, *A Heavy Feather*, and I'm ashamed to say it sold only 1100 or 1200 copies. I think Barker is one of the most unusual writers I've ever read. I hope to add her next book to our list. It isn't that I want to drop Barker from our list. I can only do her next book when financially I know I can publish it despite the fact that I may lose on it. I can do that only because I know I'll be making money on some of my art or architecture books to cover the losses. That's how I think of adding fiction and poetry writers to my list—to fit them in when I have a little money, knowing I can lose. The fact is that Barker was published by two or three other houses—large ones—before she came to me. They dropped her because they couldn't sell enough copies of her books. So even if they had *A Heavy Feather*, they wouldn't have sold many more copies than I sold. I could have given it perhaps all my attention, but I doubt very much whether it would have sold any more copies than it did with those large houses that also published Barker's books.

Interviewer: Are you saying that money is also not the answer to selling books—even good ones? That there are limits to what the sales and marketing apparatus is capable of achieving?

Braziller: If we're talking about serious literature, yes. One of the mistakes we made in the past was the undue excitement that we would have about a book, believing that if we really went out and spent money and advertised and overprinted and did all the big, big things, then perhaps we could break through and make some money on it. We'd find that was not the case. I've come to believe that a work of literature will reach that audience that just simply wants to respond to it. Beyond that, you cannot hope for more. Another thing I strongly believe is that certain works are right for certain periods. It may be that the nature of the writing or subject matter is such that the public isn't ready for that kind of writing, and this happens to be the case with each generation. I think it was Gertrude

Stein who said that each generation has its own set of problems, its own little headaches, tastes, attitudes, and that there's nothing you can do about it. I'm convinced of it. Many years ago, Alfred Knopf published some of the outstanding writers from Europe, and those books didn't sell more than 1500-2000 copies each, and we know the story of Faulkner, that his first three or four novels were remaindered by Random House. So any writer is a victim of the generation he's writing for. Getting back to the question of how I keep going publishing these writers, I just juggle with my list to enable me to make it to the next list. I know it sounds naive or idealistic, but I know you can't make money with the attitudes and ideas I have about what I want to publish. I don't even think of a breakeven point on a novel. Profit has never been my main incentive. The fact that I've been going for 25 years is the most rewarding thing of all.

Interviewer: Yet the economics of surviving as a small publisher are much different from what they were when you started out in 1955. You've recently undertaken some drastic cost-cutting measures, including pruning your staff, consolidating your office space into smaller quarters and, in general, watching your operating and overhead costs more carefully than ever before. Have you ever given thought to selling the company?

Braziller: In the latter part of the '70s there were one or two offers. While they were not too tempting, I paid attention to them, and I believe that if I could have worked something out I might have agreed to sell. But nothing came of it, and I don't think we were the kind of house that a lot of the big publishers would have been interested in. We were just too small for them.

Interviewer: Would one of the main problems have been the lack of working capital—that your financial base was considered inadequate from the point of view of prospective buyers?

Braziller: Yes, the company was never properly financed. The working capital was never there. It was always more or less functioning on contracts that I had signed with foreign publishers, getting money in advance, and that was one part of it. As a result of being underfinanced we were always faced with the problem of advances. I don't believe that in any one given period in 25 years as a publisher I had more than 10 contracts out. We just could not afford to give advances. If you take a modest advance of say, $3000, to a reasonable one of $15,000, then multiply that by 10 authors, you can see it suddenly becomes anywhere from $30,000 to $150,000. That's a lot of money you have to put out. At one time I heard that Doubleday had as much as $3- to $4-million out in advances. Now that gives you an idea of how necessary working capital is to publish currently as well as to plan ahead for the next few years.

Interviewer: How did you have to adjust your publishing operation to continue doing the books you've been doing in spite of the difficulties that resulted from the downturn in the economy beginning in the late '70s?

Braziller: I don't feel that because of our overhead, or cost of operation, we will add books just for the sake of adding books. If I have to do 10 books this spring, that's all we're going to do. Now the question is, can I survive? Can I stay in business, publishing so few books? Well, I'm not sure. And I face that problem as the days and weeks go by. But somehow it has been the method I've applied over the past 25 years. Even at the peak of our publishing program, when we had about 18 people on staff and were doing 40 books a year, it was the same. And we have never gone beyond 40 books in any given year.

Interviewer: When was the peak?

Braziller: Oh, in 1974. I think that held for every publishing house in America. Everything went. No matter what you published, more or less, you managed. In those years, we did close to $2-million in business. Today we are doing some $1,200,000 with less than a dozen people on staff. We have been affected by the changes in the industry as much as everyone else. But in our situation, we're not faced with the necessity of expansion. We never think, "Are we going ahead this year or behind?" We simply start with the premise that we're trying to get the very best books that we can and then we try to figure out how to do it.

Interviewer: You never had the benefit of the kind of formal schooling we'd expect of a publisher. In fact, you never graduated from high school but went on to become a successful businessman by age 30 and then a publisher at 40. How is it that you gravitated toward some quite specialized fields—medieval art and experimental literature, for example?

Braziller: I wonder what would have happened to my whole attitude towards the world had I gone on to college after finishing high school or gone to graduate school and become a specialist in one thing. I have met many specialists, especially in the field of art. They never budge from their particular period in their entire lives. For me, it was the opposite. I have never been one to say, I've been here before. Everything is like a new day—it's a beginning. You spend a lifetime learning, and the process never ends. The first time I went to a museum, it was to the Museum of Modern Art. I was 17 or 18. I saw a painting by Vincent Van Gogh. It was a painting of figures with picks and shovels digging potatoes. I responded because I was working for WPA with a pick and shovel at the time. When I went to Paris and discovered the *nouveau roman*, it was the same thing—literally a revelation. It was the anti-novel. I felt as if I were looking at an abstract painting. When I pick up Sarraute's most recent work, *Do You Hear Them?*, it's the same thing. I still find each of her books a remarkable achievement, even though some would say the anti-novel is dead. We're publishing Irish writers now, a new generation. Well, one could say, what's new? Fortunately I never read all of Yeats or Joyce, and if I did, would I have said: There's nothing left to be said in Irish literature after Joyce? That's the thing—to have that capacity, that willingness to give of yourself . . . as if you're looking at or reading something for the first time.

Interviewer: Would you say, then, that your underlying motive is to publish what's new?

Braziller: Of course, but I think that's closer to a philosophy or an attitude, a pleasure or a purpose that a publisher should have. And I like to feel that I'm in that category. That doesn't mean that if an established writer were to come to us, it wouldn't give me a great deal of pleasure—but not nearly as much as the constant pursuit of that silly question: Is there something new?

Interviewer: When you founded the publishing house, had you an idea of whom you might be publishing books for? Were there other publishers you looked to as models?

Braziller: No, no. My audience was myself. I had a belief that there were people out there interested in good things. What I reflect more or less as a publisher is what other individual publishers over the last 40 or 50 years have represented—an individual way of publishing.

For example, before I started in publishing, I remember going to London and I visited maybe 20 or 30 publishers. And when you went in those years, you visited individuals. There was a Victor Gollancz, a Hamish Hamilton, a Sir Stanley Unwin. There were names without any corporate structure. You met the individuals and spoke with them and after a while it was clear that the kind of books each published reflected the individual. Publishing when I began was simply one individual thinking that he wanted to do something that would show his own personal taste. That impressed me enormously, and when I came back, we also had names here in America. There was a Harold Guinzburg at Viking, an Alfred Knopf, a Bennett Cerf and there was a Mr. Simon, a Mr. Schuster. Individuals. Like anything else, the individuals are there to decide and to be responsible for something. To be responsible doesn't mean that some of those publishers didn't publish what one would perhaps call trash. But they were held responsible.

Interviewer: But you're still here, publishing by what you would call "the individual method," and all those others, the Guinzburgs and the Simons and Schusters, are no longer running companies. Why do you continue operating in this apparently obsolete style?

Braziller: I never wanted to be a big publisher because I knew that even if I could have been one, clearly, that meant giving up too much. The bigger you are, the more people you have around you and the more you give up. You have to, because people around you need the opportunity to develop in their own way. I was frightened by that—by the thought that I might end up working for them. The other publishers were getting older. They had estate and tax problems. It was the competition mainly to hold and obtain new authors that resulted in their looking for additional capital. It's a growth thing that trapped them and forced them in another direction—no, it didn't force them, they chose it—to become bigger and more competitive. The moment you take on added personnel, you have to publish more books and *then* you need money.

Interviewer: The nature of your books is such that one would think you had in-house expertise for the specialized titles—the architecture books, the social science titles, especially the medieval art books. Yet you have never hired specialist editors. How do you go about publishing the more academic titles without you yourself or an in-house editor having the expertise?

Braziller: Well, my books are not necessarily geared for a specialized audience. My method has been to get the most qualified people in the field to write on the subject for a general audience. Some of the scholars we approached have been dubious. In the case of the medieval manuscript program, some didn't think our presentation of an introduction and explanatory text was the right way to introduce the works to a general audience. A book on Persian painting, for instance, may have been addressed first to the art market or to students and then beyond that, if there's interest from the public, that's fine. But the book is nothing light or frivolous. I've always tried to straddle the two markets, to have one foot in the clear, serious, qualified market; and the other in a broad public. You can get hurt as a publisher because it's in a gray area. We don't do any marketing. We don't do any research. We don't check things out. We just do it. We do it by simply saying we feel we have the best person qualified to write the book and then we say there will be an audience for it. And if there isn't, we have no regrets. Do we get hurt financially? Yes, we do. Do we try to overcome it in some way? We try. If we succeed, we'll continue with that philosophy. If we fail, we'll be out of business. So far I've had 25 years of fun doing exactly what I wanted to do.

— **Stella Dong**

Maurice Girodias

THE OLYMPIA PRESS
8, Rue de Nesle, Paris 6ᵉ

Maurice Girodias: Perils of the Princely Pornographer

There was a time, a dozen years ago and more, when Maurice Girodias was branded the "King of Porn." He was the publisher of those green-covered paperbacks of the Olympia Press, sporadically banned on two sides of the Atlantic. By the time he moved his business to New York in the late 1960s the racy novels were alternately damned, cheered and ferreted under store counters as the "little dirties." Today they bear big prices for collectors of erotica when found in any condition at your local rare book shop.

Girodias doesn't sell them anymore. Instead he is selling his haunting, authentic life chronicle, in French and English. Crown Publishers (New York) issued the first volume in this country in November, 1980, with the title *The Frog Prince*. A slur, perhaps? If so, is Girodias jeering at his native France, or at the reckless years he passed there, or at something he feels he has become? Perhaps all three. But *The Frog Prince* is a delicious book to read. Girodias won't mind at all if you buy it and laugh.

His father was Jack Kahane, a British Jew who made a tidy fortune in his native Manchester, married the aristocratic Marcelle Girodias and settled permanently in the suburbs of Paris after World War I. Kahane never recovered from his military experience. A German gas attack left him permanently debilitated and beseiged with respiratory ailments. He lived in an idler's way for most of his years, with all of Paris as his toy. He practiced no religion and tithed to no idols but loose women, fine food, good wines and expensive tailored clothes. His wife kept most of her knowledge of Kahane's "business matters" locked away in some hard wood chest behind her ego and what must have been boundless love of husband and children.

One of those was Maurice, born in the spring of 1919 and named for his mother's brother, killed in action during the war. The author of *The Frog Prince* only saw photos of his dead uncle and seems to believe, as his spiritualist mother did, that he is the reincarnation of his namesake—MAURICE GIRODIAS. Indeed, Girodias is a mystic. One of the mauve threads woven through *The Frog Prince* is his devotion to a secret Theosophical Society in Paris during the 1930s, a coven with political intentions which demanded such disciplines of its young members as vegetarianism—and *chastity*. Maurice never suffered from the dictates of vegetarianism, beyond the ridicule of his father. Kahane never stopped his son from doing anything but he rarely approved, either, And chastity? Chastity! Therein was the curse of Maurice's life, as he fell in and out of love and carried a white-hot torch for Laurette, the lovely siren who served as understudy and spirit medium for the head of the mystical *ashram*. The cult leader, Vivian du Mas, Girodias paints as a tyrannical buffoon and power-hungry fascist who sought to mobilize the youth of Europe into a world government from underground, always several steps behind his counterpart, Adolf Hitler, whose army steamrolled over France near the close of *The Frog Prince*. Girodias's recounting of the Nazi occupation of Paris is electric and cinematic. No other author has captured it in words with such spark and sound and pace.

Maurice's existence was emotionally and intellectually distant from his father's. Had it not been for a common literary direction, father and son might scarcely have spoken to one another. In his frequent periods of illness, Jack Kahane wrote merry novels, published in London and New York by Brentano's, Inc.—*Laugh and Grow Rich* (1923) and *The Browsing Goat* (1929). Then, in 1930, Kahane founded the infamous Obelisk Press of Paris. Its purpose was to publish erotic fiction in English—novels spurned or feared by Establishment publishers—and sell them in cheap paperbound editions to tourists and to dealers in England and America who dared to sell them. Kahane wrote many of the Obelisk books himself under noms de plume—one of the most desired was *Daffodil*—but his little publishing house is best remembered for discovering expatriates like Henry Miller and Lawrence Durrell. Obelisk Press first published *Tropic of Cancer, Black Spring, Tropic of Capricorn* and the other early books of Henry Miller, plus the sub rosa novels of Miller's comrades Anais Nin and Durrell. Kahane bought the rights to *My Life and Loves* from his friend Frank Harris and kept that "banned" four-volume romp in print for years after Harris's death in 1931. As a publisher, Kahane was fearless. He issued *The Well of Loneliness*, Radclyffe Hall's roundly cursed lesbian novel, and other between-the-wars classics of the literary underground. All this, when Paris was relatively an open city and the French government so chaotic that the masses were nearly deaf to the sound of goose-stepping boots from the east. Such was the literary heritage of Maurice, son of Jack Kahane, who took his mother's last name on a faked I.D. card when Paris fell to the Third Reich. By then, Kahane had succumbed to his rotting lungs and died in dread fear of the Nazis, in September, 1939. His father's passing is the denouement of *The Frog Prince*. The book closes with an illicit tryst under the noses of the S.S. in Occupied France—and a lusty, happy look ahead. Girodias tells us that the closing year was 1942. He was 23 years old.

In *The Frog Prince*, Girodias presents himself as a foolish young man with a good heart and uncontrolled sexual passions which he cannot fulfill, half out of inhibition and half out of the chastity pledge to the crazy Theosophist *ashram*. He falls in and out of love with *jeunes filles* and always returns from solo adventures—flights from his own passion—to the sisterly warmth of Laurette, the light of his life, who refuses his love and sensuality out of her devotion to the "Cause" of that mountebank guru Vivian. Girodias laughs at himself, at governments, at his father, his friends, his father's famous writing friends—and he made us laugh at them. But is *The Frog Prince* the real Maurice Girodias? We wanted to know that. He agreed to see us in the conference room of Crown Publishers in New York City.

Girodias was, as he declared himself "an active and conscious pornographer," analogous to Picasso in that he crisscrossed periods and movements in erotica. Kahane had exposed him to *fin de siecle* decadence—Baudelaire and Oscar Wilde and their disciples of the gaslight era—and that age's sole survivor by 1930, Frank Harris. Girodias added on the outrageous mysticism and perverse sexual frolics of such writing shamans as Aleister Crowley, "The Great Beast" who led a blind cult following till his death in 1947 and infuriated scholars by writing and self-publishing steamy fictions, attributing them to famous authors long dead. (The famous example is Crowley's *White Stains*, falsely credited to London poet Ernest Dowson.) Then, when Girodias inaugurated his Olympia Press in 1953 for the new crop of bohemian expatriates in Paris, he furnished victuals and victories to what came to be called the Beat Generation. In this crucial connection, Girodias and his Olympia Press were bread and butter for the likes of William S. Burroughs—whose *Naked Lunch* made its first appearance in the Olympia line in 1959—and Beat poet

Gregory Corso, whose only novel, *The American Express*, surfaced with the green Olympia jacket in 1961. Then there are the modern literary lions who owe their lionization to Girodias: Jean Genet, Samuel Beckett, J.P. Donleavy (*The Ginger Man*), Nikos Kazantzakis (*Zorba the Greek* first came off Olympia's line as *Alexis Zorba*), and the late ingrate Vladimir Nabokov, whose *Lolita* would never have become a world classic had not Girodias accepted and published it in 1955, only to be slandered and disowned by the irascible and academically accepted Nabokov soon afterward.

And then there are those contemporary "bad books" of international sensation, for which credit is due to Girodias—*Story of O*, Chester Himes' *Pinktoes*, the English versions of the works of De Sade, Terry Southern's *Candy*, etc., etc.—but more anon.

Girodias was a legend in Paris and New York for more than a generation, always spending beyond his means, dressing as his father had taught in the finest men's threads, a dandy courting ruin and infamy with a cavalier gusto and Left Bank elan. We expected to meet just such a proud, laughing peacock. We were introduced to someone quite other than that, and more. He was some 20 minutes late for our appointment and somberly apologetic. He wore no expensive suit or hat—just a tweed jacket, open collar and no tie at his throat, and doffed a storm coat against the year-end New York weather. His lush head of wavy dark hair has gone silver grey. His eyes are very brown, almost black, and they burn more with anger than amorous mischief. His Gallic features are finely chiseled and fit for statuary. Albeit he is married to Lilla Lyon, of the aristocratic Cabot line of New England, he could still win hearts on two continents and doubtless will, in whatever measure.

We chatted with Maurice Girodias alone, first at Crown and later at a cocktail lounge near Penn Station, for nearly three hours. His low voice is wistful, his accent very Parisian, his speech mellifluous, his manners calm and urbane. He is quite the international city dweller. Moreover, he has the international celebrity's dislike of *papperazzi*. He allowed us to photograph him but he is troubled by camera flashes. We offered to cease and desist but he smiled and waved us on. "Go ahead," he mumbled. "It's all part of the job."

The Frog Prince is his English version of *J'arrive!* which came out in Paris in 1977 from a publisher named Stock. It is the first of the three planned parts of *Une Journee Sur la Terre*, its main title, which Girodias told us is not adequately translatable into English. The second part, *Cause Celebre*, is due in about a year. The third book, which could be the most unusual of all, is tentatively titled

Girodias 33

Departs. We asked him about this autobiographical project. What prompted him to write it?

"It was as I said in the opening pages of *The Frog Prince*," he said. "I was talked into writing my life story by my old friend John Calder. It served as self-analysis. Better than paying the man who sits behind you with a pipe in his mouth! When I was persuaded to write it I was in a bad state of mind. And I certainly needed the money. I was very broke, again! In the beginning it was difficult, as the opening part shows. Afterward it seemed to flow freely, of its own volition. People I had forgotten came back to me, like ghosts. My father—I found I had never really known him. All of the people are real. None of the names were changed. I wrote more for the first volume but I decided to save it for the second."

We wondered if he had changed *J'arrive!* any, for the version called *The Frog Prince*. "Yes," Girodias said. "Three friends of mine translated the book for me. I read the transcript and didn't like it at all anymore. So I rewrote the book in English in a matter of three weeks. Some of the writing was difficult. I found myself using words unusual even in English works. And I experienced much internal struggle. But how can you learn about yourself and your hopes and your ideas, except by looking back, by weighing the past? This was another of my principal aims. So in effect it is an underground history of my mind. I discovered that I never knew what my father meant to me, and all that he made me. And I recall all those others, like poor, funny Gregor (a son of Russian expatriates who was a teen-age friend of Girodias's, and is described as ugly, gluttonous, Rabelaisian and a born cynic). You say Gregor was your favorite character? He was surely one of mine!"

Did the Paris edition, *J'arrive!*, have illustrations? "No," he said, "but I wanted them."

We asked about the next two volumes—what will be in them?

"The next volume will be about the war years and after, and the troubles I had as a publisher. I started the Obelisk Press again after the war. How it was taken away from me, and how I started again with Olympia in 1953, and other business ventures, is a great story in my next volume. I have already begun to write it. There are many colorful people to talk about. And the third volume will be set in the year 2000—how I see myself then, and the future of the world."

He told us that *Cause Celebre* will have the same title here and in France. As things look to him now, Crown will be his American publisher. "Most American publishers refused to consider *The Frog*

Prince because they continued to see me as an adversary. I had taken dares in the past, on books fearful to them. So had my father. And as it is, *The Frog Prince* treats phases of history in a manner like no book before. For example, who has ever described the German occupation of Paris and the fear of the people as I did? With Crown Publishers I was very fortunate. They have been good to me."

While reading *The Frog Prince* we could find no special enthusiasm in Girodias for the work of his father. We wondered if it had really been his intention to continue the productions of the Obelisk Press. "Oh yes!" he answered. "It was a family tradition! Early in life I thought I wanted to draw and paint. Sometimes I do." It was the 14-year-old Maurice Girodias, in fact, who drew the cover for the first edition of Henry Miller's *Tropic of Cancer* (1934).

We had also noticed a certain spoofing of such notable friends of Jack Kahane's as Henry Miller and Lawrence Durrell, as Girodias presents them in *The Frog Prince*—and although he celebrates the badinage of his father with Frank Harris, the author of *My Life and Loves* never appears. "I always admired Henry Miller," Girodias commented to us. "He always fascinated me. He was sly and in many ways a coward. Even in this country he feared that the Ku Klux Klan or someone would try to burn his house down. I was too young to have ever met Frank Harris. Though I never saw Harris, I made a point of keeping his *My Life and Loves* in print for as long and as often as I could. When my father bought the rights to the four volumes, I was constantly amused by Harris's cockiness and arrogance in the books—the way he would write one chapter in mock seriousness, and the one right after in fantastic storytelling about his impossible sex adventures. He was a delight to read. I suppose I felt I knew him."

And what of Laurette, the girl of his youthful dreams who was the stewardess, spirit medium and probably concubine of the magus Vivian? "I courted Laurette for ten years," Girodias told us. "We were married for three years and it burned out. We were not good to each other. I think of her now as an old woman. But she is the mother of my children. The line of creation goes on."

During the war, when the Nazis were the overlords of France, Girodias stowed away what remained of the Obelisk Press and established Les Editions du Chene, a publishing house for expensive art books. We asked him if the Nazis ever harassed him during the occupation. "No," he said. "Les Editions du Chene published very lavish art books with little or no text. The Nazis were not troubled by books with no text or very little print. The rise of Nazism in Europe was due to the suppression of free speech and free press.

Hitler's dictates necessitated it. After the war I revived the Obelisk Press as a division of Les Editions du Chene. Later it was taken away from me by my enemies and Les Editions du Chene was sold to the big publisher, Hachette. It still exists today."

We asked Girodias if any of the obscenity prosecutions against him in France had been mere subterfuges for politically motivated liquidations, as so many of the classic obscenity cases in the U.S. have proven to be. "Yes," he admitted. "I published pamphlets about the black market Mafia, just after the war. High government officials and corrupt practices were named." At the time—1946 and 1947— Harris's *My Life and Loves* and Miller's *Tropic of Cancer* were top-of-the-line items from Obelisk. Girodias commented years later that these paperbacks were an education for American G.I.'s stationed in Europe. The upshot for Girodias himself was *l'affaire Miller*—the suppression of Miller's works in English and in French (translations by Maurice's brother Eric, now a cattle rancher in South America) and the loss of Les Editions du Chene, including the old family company, Obelisk. By 1950, Maruice Girodias was left with nothing.

What followed was a period of drunkenness and dissipation for Girodias and his brother Eric. For three years they lived like beggars and derelicts. His marriage to Laurette had ended. Girodias credits his re-entry into human society to the controversial Bogomoletz cure —a series of injections of monkey glands. The physiological shock allegedly cleaned his system of alcoholism and the phantoms of abject depression. His health restored—however it happened—Girodias reopened for business in spring, 1953, as the Olympia Press. The first book offered for sale in the new series was Henry Miller's *Plexus*. So began what was surely the golden age of the Frog Prince.

"I like William Burroughs very much," he told us. "A kind gentleman. I met Norman Mailer in the mid-1950s. A nice, brilliant fellow. I remember him as a pudgy little man. And yes, I met Samuel Roth (of the landmark Roth obscenity decision in the U.S. Supreme Court, 1957). Roth was in Paris. I was introduced by that crazy Gershon Legman, at a restaurant. Legman used to hang around the Olympia offices in the front section where we sold books." Legman, foremost scholar of erotica, had worked for Roth in New York in the early 1950s, when Roth's books and magazines were upsetting the police, the Postmaster General, the Kefauver Committee, the FBI, and Walter Winchell.

The troubles awaiting Sam Roth were also in store for Girodias in Paris. Other than Henry Miller and the big-name authors whose reputations were ultimately assured on the vehicle of Olympia Press,

Maurice Girodias tapped the bohemian talent pool responsible for *Merlin*, a quarterly lit-mag published in English by a pack of British Beats living in Paris. Those writers turned out piles of sexy novels for Olympia, most of them by-lined on the green covers with pseudonyms made up by Girodias himself. One of the most prolific was John Coleman, whose pen name became famous among horny readers everywhere: "Marcus Van Heller." An Olympia scribe of many names was a Frenchman, Michel Gall, who wrote *The Sexual Life of Robinson Crusoe* (Girodias gave as the author, "Humphrey Richardson") and *A Bedside Odyssey* (the cover gives the authorship to "Homer & Associates"). Another Olympia "regular" of prodigious output was the artist Norman Rubington, whose many books Girodias adorned with the shivery by-line of "Akbar Del Piombo."

Many of the real identities of his authors—those who haven't revealed themselves already or become famous since the Olympia days—Girodias refused to tell us. Some of them wrote books that became cultural phenomena and distinguished Olympia's list of "little dirties" in extraordinary ways.

Item: In 1958, Girodias issued a novel from the Obelisk days, *The Gaudy Image*, signed with the pseudonym "William Talsman." Obelisk had had difficulties exporting this one into the U.S. because of its homosexual theme. "William Talsman was a college student in the American Midwest when he wrote *The Gaudy Image*," Girodias told us. "I understand that he is now deceased, but I still won't tell you his real name, whether it could hurt his memory or not. I published *The Gaudy Image* because I felt it had great merit among homosexual novels."

Item: In 1954, Girodias published *Story of O*, first sold as fiction by an anonymous author. Over the next decade the book became a soft-core classic. It became so immensely popular in the English-speaking world that legions of readers, critics and police chiefs demanded to know who the author was. Many in France believed that Girodias himself had written it. *Story of O* was reissued with the by-line "Pauline Reage." The world then puzzled over who Pauline Reage might be. "I have never met the author of *Story of O*," Girodias told us. "I know her real name but I am sworn to secrecy and cannot reveal it. I can tell you authoritatively that the author is a woman who has since written sequels to *Story of O*, published only in French.[1] Anyone who is familiar with her books, taken together, could discover her real identity." That is his last word on the subject.

Olympia Press managed as well to add durable curiosities to the history of erotic literature. One of those was the apocryphal "Fifth Volume" of Frank Harris's *My Life and Loves*. In the mid-1950s, Girodias approached the attorney for Harris's aging widow, Nellie, asking a price for the unpublished volume. He had heard of such a manuscript since the time when his father had bought rights to the other four parts. The wizened old solicitor admitted that the manuscript existed, and that Nellie Harris had been offered a large sum by a major French publisher. Girodias offered a boisterous one million francs, signed a contract and left the lawyer's office with what worked out to be a sheaf of articles Harris had intended for magazines! Ripped off? "The 'Fifth Volume' was only 50 manuscript pages," Girodias laughed. "I took it to my friend Alexander Trocchi, who used it to write a wonderful Frank Harris pastiche for me. We sold it as *The Fifth Volume* and later as *What Frank Harris Did Not Say*. When Grove Press published the complete and unexpurgated *My Life and Loves*, 'Five Volumes in One,' in 1963, they used only the 50 manuscript pages as their fifth volume."

Another tour de force was the "completed" version of Aubrey Beardsley's *Under the Hill*. The famous English artist of the gaslight era had never finished this saucy rococo tale. After Beardsley's death in 1898, his wily publisher, Leonard Smithers, offered an edition of *Under the Hill* with the famous Beardsley drawings. In 1958, the Canadian expatriate poet John Glassco arrived at Girodias's office in Paris with his own manuscript of *Under the Hill*. Glassco had first read it as a Halderman-Julius Little Blue Book in his teen years and had always wished to finish the story himself. And here it was. "I can't imagine how Halderman-Julius found the text in the first place," Girodias remarked to us. "But I was personally entranced by the Beardsley story and especially his fine illustrations for it." The Olympia Press edition of *Under the Hill* became a sleeper, and sold well again when Grove Press bought it in the 1960s.

Detractors have repeatedly implied that Girodias wrote many of his Olympia Press books himself and attached oddball pseudonyms to them. He claims no such authorship. "I wrote one other book, on Roger Casement, the Irish revolutionary," he admitted to us. "But I don't like it now. The style is bad. Too scholarly. Grove Press published it (*The Black Diaries of Roger Casement*, 1959) and it sold perhaps a dozen copies. It was unpopular as a book in its time, because Casement was presented as a homosexual hero."

Girodias got into real trouble in France when he showed the government of Charles De Gaulle that he wasn't just a one-trick pony. *Lolita* had made such a windfall for Olympia Press that Girodias moved his offices to 7 rue Saint-Severin, a large old building, in 1957. Below the offices he opened La Grande Severine, an elegant restaurant with four different clubs. In the cellar he opened a theater where, in 1964, he staged an adaptation of De Sade's *The Bedroom Philosophers*. The Paris police raided the theater and closed La Grande Severine. Girodias went to trial on obscenity charges for several books in the Olympia line, plus the activities at his night club. By early 1965 he had lost La Grande Severine and just barely salvaged Olympia Press. He announced that he would leave France. Civil rights attorney Charles Rembar claimed (in his book, *The End of Obscenity*) that he suggested to Girodias, at a cocktail party, that he move to the U.S. He did come, arriving in New York in 1967.

"*The New York Times* continues to publish that boyish photograph of me from the time I arrived here!" Girodias remarked to me. "Newspapers have a lot of power. They play with facts and sell them as truth. They help to promote Puritanical attitudes across classes, both here and in France."

Girodias has frequently compared his legal troubles in France, under the various regimes, with the prosecutions of Flaubert's *Madame Bovary* when it first appeared in 1857, and Baudelaire's *Les Fleurs du Mal* when its second, larger edition went on sale in 1861. He sees himself as a victim, first of all, of class struggle as that struggle is stoked and fanned by moronic governments. The object of class manipulation, he believes, is mind control. We asked him if the class war is as bad in his native land as it has been here.

"It's horrible!" he said. "The bourgeois class is as arrogant and small-minded in France as it is here—or more so. Their representatives are capable of enacting oppressive laws as bad as or worse than the fascists. You can think of it in Orwellian terms. After a while you cannot tell one side from the other. Giscard D'Estaing's government has brought with it much of a pall on culture in France. Much apathy. And De Gaulle's time was one of frustration and bitterness in the community of the artistic and cultural avant-garde. My wife and I live in New York and in Paris. But Paris isn't as exciting now as I recall it. I lived on the Left Bank for many years. What I see there now is a degree of stagnation. We left Boston for similar reasons. Boston is a very bad place."

We were still on the subject of cultural stagnation and class manipulation when we reminded Girodias of his own account of French fascists in the 1930s who sought to enforce press censorship on the faked-up rationale of protecting "the family." We pointed out that the New Right and bunk-shooting TV evangelists are using the same ploy to influence legislators toward a new wave of censorship in the U.S. "It is always used," Girodias commented. "It is a trick to effect mind control and stifle free expression. The object is to invent new 'truths' under the guise of safeguards, as newspapers and magazines often do. As for the Moral Majority, it will likely be ignored and eventually forgotten."

By the time he had established Olympia Press in New York during the 1960s, Girodias had already made some good friends there. "Barney Rosset (founder of Grove Press) and I became very good friends in Paris and New York. I introduced him to Henry Miller. And I knew the gentlemen of Citadel Press. My favorites were Allan Wilson—a very pleasant, learned fellow who knew the theater—and Phil Foner. The others at Citadel seemed clownish and lacking in polish." (Citadel Press was eventually bought by Lyle Stuart, who has also distinguished himself as a publisher of erotica. Girodias had some arrangements with Stuart several years ago, but told us that they proved to be counter-productive.)

Olympia Press continued from New York into the early '70s, even adding a division, Ophelia Press, as an imprint for what Girodias considered "heavier, more intense books." Eventually his business faltered and died. "The book pirates of the West Coast really brought down Olympia Press forever," he told us. "Among the worst were Marvin Miller (Collectors Publications) and that other scoundrel in San Diego who first pirated *Candy*."

Will Maurice Girodias go back into publishing? "Yes," he told us. "But I hope to diversify into very different publishing ventures. Not just erotica, and maybe none at all. And I don't wish to involve myself in those old matters of business and distribution and so on. My interests are literary. And I want to set up a number of publishing outlets for a number of different kinds of books—and manage them from afar."

Sort of a holding company for publishers? "Yes," he said. "Exactly."

Maurice Girodias is, first and last, the cultural anarchist whom he self-caricatured in *The Frog Prince*. "Freedom of expression is the basis for everything worthwhile in life," he stressed to us. "Free speech and free press are all that we can base our future upon. I distrust all political systems and class struggles because of the threats they pose to those freedoms."

—William F. Ryan

[1] *Return to the Chateau* was published in English by Grove Press in 1971.

David Godine

An Interview with David Godine

David R. Godine is a respected, adventurous, out-spoken publisher and a *soi-disant* cultural elitist. On a staff of ten, he runs his small and surprisingly successful, young house—David R. Godine Press—from the basement of a shabby genteel, backbay Boston mansion, organized, as he puts it, as a "participatory dictatorship." Since Godine set up shop ten years ago on family capital, the annual list has grown to forty titles—or what one journalist recently described as .0001 per cent of America's annually published books. But what sets the Godine fraction apart from most others is his unflinching commitment to the highest standards, with respect to content *and* production.

In a publishing era plagued by conglomerate financing, increasing bureaucratic specialization, high-rolling agents, prefabricated bestsellers, seven-figure advances, the media "blitz," and paperbacks that fall apart in one reading, the Godine Press is something of an anomaly. Godine's house is independent and small—in size though not in scope—and essentially intends to stay that way. Hating agents and avoiding big money promotion, Godine relies instead on the intrinsic quality of his books, good and prominent reviews, word-of-mouth advertising, and a healthy relationship with a range of bookshops that regularly stand by him. His books, some of the few in the country to carry a colophon, reveal a meticulous attention to the quality of paper (invariably acid-free), bindings (always sewn, even on the paperbacks), type-face, type-setting and design. The care taken with production shows too in the judiciously selected and deliberately eclectic range of books he publishes—art, photography, chapbooks, history, fiction, and inexpensive, hardbound editions of poetry. How he has managed this hat-trick—quality content, quality production, *and* increasing market acceptability during a recession—is something of a mystery. With the mannered cultivation of the theatrically iconoclastic, Godine offers his own explanation: "I'll tell you a well-kept secret in publishing. If you publish good books and keep your expectations within the bounds of reality and run a fairly tight ship, you're going to make money—there's no way not to. But if you build a house of trash, some day it will burn."

This kind of go-ahead prescription doesn't account for how Godine has succeeded so much as it simply reiterates the fact that he has done so. But the aggressiveness and bluntness reveal more than they say. Godine is a master of the re-tooled cliche, the pithy and promotional aphorism, which shows in his glib—and sometimes meretricious—desire to surprise. Taking aim at one of his *betes noires*—technology and its deleterious effects on the aesthetics of publishing—Godine will say: "One of the prime rules of life is that as technology improves, aesthetics deteriorates. Speed substitutes for quality. Invention is the mother of problems." Part of the secret of Godine's success is his straight-forward self-promotion and disarming conceit.

But part of it too is his anarchronistic commitment to the nuts and bolts of his trade. Godine studied typography at Dartmouth, bibliography at Oxford, and print-making with the artist Leonard Baskin, and since his teens has been a devoted collector of fine books, passionate about the refinements in production and design. This background and an almost renaissance affection for the art of printing (indeed Godine believes that 'the most glorious books ever produced were produced in France between 1520 and 1550' in monotype) show as much in the books Godine publishes as in their peerless quality. The current list includes two works on calligraphy *and* the classical alphabets alone, and the writers and artists to whom Godine is typically attracted demonstrate the same cultivated attitude toward their craft as Godine himself, whether it be William Gass's conscientious love of words or Jill Krementz's rigorous respect for the photographic image. Put these two together—the arrogant pushiness of Madison Avenue and the old world commitment to quality—and you have something of the secret of Godine's success.

Nevertheless, Godine's bullish iconoclasm shatters even the conventional image of the iconoclast. Talking with him the other day overlooking Grand Central Station from the potted-palm lounge of the New York City Yale Club, it was clear that if the Godine Press offers any kind of alternative to the commercial quagmire of most publishing today, it's still no simple question of David versus Goliath.

Interviewer: In the American book business, the David Godine Press has a reputation as a serious, quality publisher providing an alternative to a trade characterized by a variety of ills. Nevertheless, looking over your list, it's difficult to see what makes Godine special. You publish little fiction, for instance, and fiction, especially the literary novel, is in more trouble than any other kind of book today. If the Godine Press is doing so few novels, how can anyone claim that it is satisfying any of the current needs in publishing?

Godine: We don't pretend to be and we never claimed that we were. We satisfy other needs. For serious criticism, where we publish Sullivan, Gass, and Nemerov. For serious books of photography, art, and history. For serious books for children. Children's publishing, for example, has traditionally aimed at the lowest common denominator; we try for the highest (a child is not going to read Dylan Thomas for fun; but you might read it to your children for fun because it's more fun for you to read Thomas than googa). Also we satisfy a need for serious books from other countries: we do a great many translations. In the current spring list, we have a six hundred page novel by Ernesto Sabato that cost $8,000 just to translate. I think it's terrific and hope it gets a front page review. But that's a risk: the kind of risk you take with a serious, eclectic list; not the kind of risk you take with a list consisting of books about duck decoys and Martha's Vineyard.

Your question, though, puts an intellectual premium on people who write novels as opposed to people who paint or take pictures or write non-fiction, criticism, or poetry. There are always creators. That a novelist may or may not be getting hurt in the squeeze speaks more for the condition of the culture and what book buyers are willing to pay for than it does for a lack of principles within the publishing trade. It's like blaming the thermometer for the temperature.

As for fiction, Ahron Appelfeld (*Badenheim 1939*) is our boy along with Benedict Kiely and William Gass. But we don't publish much fiction.

Interviewer: Why?

Godine: Because you have to pay too much for fiction. Because it's risky. Because it's the last thing a small publisher should get into. And it's the last thing a small publisher should get into mainly because of the agent. What distinguishes publishing today from what it was thirty, forty, or fifty years ago is the presence of the agent. We deal with agents but only because of the interest we might already have in an author who happens to have an agent and basically says, "Listen, I want to do this book with Godine, make the best deal you can." That is not the same as saying, "I have to have $10,000 or no deal."

Large publishers today have no control. They have no control over their main asset—their authors—because their authors don't belong to them. They belong to agents. If the publishing house does a book poorly, the asset leaves. If it does the job well, the asset triples the asking price. The average trade publisher is rewarded only for mediocrity, not so bad the author's agent tells the author to leave, not so good they've created a star. God help anyone who relies on agents.

Interviewer: What do you think, then, of the argument that fiction is suffering because of the overall state of the publishing industry?

Godine: I think that's horseshit. The kind of anxious questions being batted around the publishing world about the "state of fiction" are really non-questions. Good fiction like bad fiction will continue to be published. If a Joseph Conrad or a William Faulkner or a Norman Mailer were out there he'd be published by a respectable press. There's no dearth of good writing, and publishers are neither so venal nor so stupid nor so short-sighted that they're not going to snap up the next John Irving. We're a small house and we must get in 90 manuscripts a week, of which maybe 89.7 are absolutely worthless. I mean, one weeps for the trees, they're that bad.

Interviewer: Sure, good fiction is getting published. But as only one, relatively constant item in lists which increase year after year, isn't there more than enough evidence of its neglect?

Godine: It's possible that an argument can be made that fewer first novels are published. But maybe that's because there are more second and third novels published. On the other hand, look at Knopf publishing 17 new novels, and that, while not typical, is a staggering number.

What is changing is the profile of the industry: the powerhouses are disappearing. Godine is not pre-eminent in its commitment to the novel, but we publish more good novels than Scribners. And that is absolutely amazing: thirty or forty years ago, Scribners was publishing every fiction writer of any consequence in the country. The house was without a rival, and could get anyone it wanted. Now, its influence is negligible.

Unfortunately, Scribners is not an exception. There are a great many publishers who, from the position of doing good fiction with good design and good editors, now publish so poorly and so diffidently that they print books in numbers of 2,500 after which they disappear. We're not so good, *really*; it's only that everyone else is so bad. We stand out not by virtue of our excellence but because there are fewer and fewer houses publishing well than there were twenty or thirty years ago.

Interviewer: What did you have in mind when you said recently that "emotionally and financially small houses struggle, but our existence is essential to readers"?

Godine: I suppose our existence could be seen as essential to readers because it is essential to writers. It's different for an author to work with a house like Godine from even a good house like Random House.

Interviewer: How?

Godine: It's more human. I'm personally involved with every book we produce. I can tell you the paper it's printed on and the type it's set in. I've read the text. I've edited a good deal of them. And the same is true of everyone in this house. That's not true of large houses. Robert Bernstein has not read every book that Random House publishes, let alone its subsidiaries Knopf and Pantheon. He's an administrator—a good one, I'm sure—but not someone who feels a compulsion to be personally involved in everything that goes out under his name—at least in the way that Alfred Knopf did or that Roger Straus does today.

We have the philosophy that good books make money and bad books don't. If you publish good books, realistically contain your expectations, and run a fairly tight ship, you're going to make money; there's no way not to.

And you can't subsidize good books with bad books. If you publish schlock, you inevitably produce it like schlock, and consequently it comes out looking like schlock. You can't look at a Doubleday list—even if you don't know anything about literature—

and really take those books seriously, even though some of them are probably serious books: they look so terrible.

Interviewer: Being involved at every level of the production of a book, would you describe yourself as an autocratic publisher? Do you initiate most of the titles?

Godine: No. Bill Goodman, an editor from Harvard University Press and Harcourt, Brace, Jovanovich, originates a lot of the books. The two front page reviews we got last year in the *New York Times* were Bill Goodman books. I had nothing to do with them, except design. A lot of the children's books are done by someone else. Our publicity manager has a book. Our receptionist has a book. I think that everybody in the company, except the people in sales, should have a book that they're responsible for. I also think it's important that people here have a feeling they have a share in the operation—that's the only way to attract good people in the first place, with the escalating demands of publishing today, although I'd like to be able to pay the people who work here more. Ultimately, I want to make the company employee-owned, like Norton.

Interviewer: Do you envision the Godine Press developing into a big house?

Godine: No. The maximum number of people should be twenty or twenty-five. And then perhaps fifty to sixty really exciting books a year. Original books, not reprints. I'd be very happy with that.

Interviewer: How are you reaching your market as, apart from what you set aside for direct mailing shots, you obviously don't have a massive advertising budget? Are your sales largely from reviews and word-of-mouth recommendations?

Godine: Very much. And bookstores: they're great allies and sell our books very aggressively.

I remember one of our early annual Halloween parties in 1973. I went over to a neighbouring silo to make sure that people weren't smoking too much. It was where we stored our unsold books. That turned out to be a moment of epiphany. We were printing beautiful books and not selling them. I resolved from that moment on that I would have to find out how to be a publisher, to put it all together—editorial, sales, marketing, all the rest of it. Until then I had just been

Godine 49

a privasher not a publisher.

To think we're out of the woods now or will be in the next five or ten years, however, is not true. Any publisher at any time can slip up. We're certainly more vulnerable than most because we have a shorter backlist; we're only less vulnerable because we employ fewer people and because our overhead is commensurately less.

But we're not stupid and we're aggressive. When you're small you have to be. You have got to go out after the Stanley Elkins of the world; they're not going to come to you. There's hardly a book in the catalogue that we didn't go out ourselves and get. And we didn't pay very much money for them because we went out and found them.

Interviewer: You have an interesting "out there" mentality towards publishing. If the market is "out there," people will buy the book; if the talent is "out there," you can find it. Is that the way you understand it? I sense that you don't see the Godine Press creating any particular tendency in writing or buying, or stimulating the development of a specific market, but rather just picking up the possibilities for sales that already exist "out there."

Godine: I hope that as we get richer we will experiment more with our list and the way we produce it. I would like to publish a few really unusual books every year, books that test and push against the conventionally accepted limitations of the form.

I do believe, however, that we are creating, if not a particular tendency in writing or buying, a particular way of producing books. The point we are trying to make again and again is this: quality books do not necessarily cost more money to make. The extra expense is not significant and will generate, we believe, extra sales. If we have a mission, it's to make people ask for truth in labelling. When a consumer buys a book, he has nowhere near the protection he has when he buys almost everything else. Buy marmalade and it says on the jar what's in it. Buy a suit and a label says what the material is. But buy a book and you won't have a clue about the way it's made or the quality of the paper or the nature of the binding.

Interviewer: There seems to be a quaint, old world dilettantism about producing quality books under today's economic conditions.

Godine: No, I don't think so. I think there is a hunger for quality in books. When a book cost $2.95 or $3.95, which they did until recently, I don't think people thought too much about it. Today a big novel costs $15 or $17.50. People are thinking how many socks or groceries $17.50 would buy. At that price, they want a book to be around for their children to read. I think that if you publish Gass, for instance, you want to produce a book that will be read for twenty-five or forty or a hundred years.

Interviewer: From what you say, it appears that you are not creating a market, but that a market will always exist for a quality book, in respect to its content and its production. Why, then, aren't there more houses like the Godine Press? Are you in a position significantly better than most because you are in Boston?

Godine: We couldn't survive in New York. The overhead would be too big, and we couldn't afford the editors or the production people or the talent. I think we'd get caught up in certain Manhattan publishing trade practices that would destroy a small press like our own. On a more basic level, my energies would be diluted managing the company and our minimal resources drained lunching and dining in New York. Also, it's easier to stay away from the professional sharks in Boston, though I don't think we'd ever be dumb enough to be prey to sharks in the first place or we wouldn't be in business. There are, moreover, a number of advantages to Boston. We have direct access to a sophisticated intellectual community, with both Harvard and MIT across the river.

Interviewer: Is this representative of a more general decentralization in American publishing? A trend away from New York?

Godine: There are advantages to being away from New York. Nevertheless, it would be difficult to be a trade publisher without regular access to New York. One of us is down here virtually every day.

Most people think of us as a specialty publisher, but we probably have more books in book clubs per list than any publisher. We do a lot of first serial rights, sub-rights; we are out to squeeze seven cents out of every nickel, marketing the copyright as an asset. We couldn't survive without New York because we do all this business here. If we were in Chicago or Des Moines we would be that much further from the source of an enormous amount of our profit.

Interviewer: In the past, you've expressed irritation at the suggestion that your own money keeps your press in business.

Godine: I am not irritated by it; it is just not true. I am irritated by the suggestion that I'm not under the same necessity to make a profit as the big publishers. My personal investment in the Press is actually very modest, and the financing is arranged in such a way that I have to make up personally anything we lose, and believe me I can't afford for that to be too much. There's been no new capital investment in the company in the past two years, and the claim that we must subsidize our books to price them so low is completely unfounded: it's hogwash.

It is true, though, that I was fortunate to have had enough capital or enough access to capital to start a press at a time when one needed only a reasonable outlay.

Interviewer: It would be harder today?

Godine: I think it's very tough today. We've built up a backlist—not comparable to that of New Directions, Pantheon, or Knopf—but a respectable backlist of a hundred titles that sell fairly reasonably. To establish that kind of list today you'd have to publish for three very expensive and difficult years doing—if you could afford it—thirty books a year. And that assumes every book's a hit, and God knows they won't be.

Interviewer: Are the economic conditions today preventing the emergence of new publishers?

Godine: It's going to be very tough to enter New York trade publishing without big dollars and big backers. There are a lot of books around for people who hustle and look for them. There are good authors around with terrific projects. But you need an organization—that is, you need to carry an overhead—that can run your company while you're out sniffing around for those books. That's the real problem for the small publisher today. The small press publisher is everything: cook, bottle washer, editor, production manager, sales manager: you get so bogged down in the details that you can't see the forest for the trees.

Interviewer: I'm wondering if the situation is any different in London. What do you think about the publishing situation in England?

Godine: It's a real mess. Again we tend to blame the industry for incompetence or over expansion. But to me the real problem in England is that people don't read. The British market—the number of people that can be relied on to buy a book—is a lot smaller than ours. Worse, the whole Commonwealth market is falling to pieces. Australia has been taken away, New Zealand has been taken away, and Canada is on its way. British publishers used to have an export market which accounted for maybe sixty per cent of an edition: now it accounts for maybe twenty: that's got to be tough.

Then there's the British typographic unions: those guys are making more money than the chief executive at Simon and Schuster. It's outrageous what they're making. And, on top of that, British publishers insist on remaining loyal enough to their "reading public" and their country to continue printing in England, and consequently they must sell books at a price that isn't competitive on an open market. The American edition of any British book is always going to be twenty to thirty per cent cheaper. Nobody's going to buy the U.K. edition, and that's got to hurt.

We're very lucky in the U.S. right now. Our dollar buys more. Our printing, paper, and binding industries are very competitive. And we've got the raw materials: it's awesome, especially compared to England, what we can choose from in raw materials.

Interviewer: Do you have many connections with British publishing?

Godine: Yeah, too many.

Interviewer: How so?

Godine: Because they always come across being so meek and mild, and whenever we make a deal with them we always get killed. Either the pound goes up or the dollar goes down or something terrible happens. It's just not a happy situation.

Interviewer: It seems, even as you talk about the problems facing British publishers, that if you have an adversary, it's technology.

Godine: I suppose. As a cultural elitist you have mass culture as an adversary. Conglomerates dominate book publishing—just as they have dominated radio and television—and the pressure for profit they impose tends to homogenize everything: not just the effort of production but what is produced. The truly excellent is regarded with a certain amount of hostility or suspicion just by virtue of its excellence or its difference.

The recent publicity about publishing has proved, if nothing else, that anybody with a reasonable amount of intelligence and perhaps a smidgen of talent can anticipate what the market wants and will pay for. But I don't think that most writers, successful or unsuccessful, really write for the market. I can't imagine Norman Mailer changing his style because he thought it would sell more copies of his book.

But, you're right, the more basic problem is simply technology. The most glorious books ever produced were produced in France between 1520 and 1550. In no other period have books been so exquisitely illustrated and made in terms of the typography, the quality of the paper, and the inventiveness of the binding. The art of printing was perfected in the 1500s and has gone steadily downhill since. Computer typesetting, for example, is no step forward over the linotype, and the linotype is no step forward over the monotype, and the monotype was basically a fast way to do hand setting. I don't believe in old techniques just for the sake of their being old, but the fact is that you look at a typeface set in linotype and compare it to the same face set in a computer system there is a world of difference in the character of the letters, the shape of the letters, the quality of the letters, and all the niceties that make for decent typography.

You can witness in Harper and Row and so many other houses like it a terrific deterioration of standards. It's not necessarily because less money per book is spent or that the cost of the material as it relates to the price of the book has increased. It's merely that what is available to a publisher today is so much more inferior to what was available twenty and thirty years ago, in respect to the reproducing technology and the people using it. One of the prime rules of our life is that as technology improves, aesthetics deteriorate.

Personally I'd love to go back to monotype if it were feasible. I'd love to. It was the best system of manufacturing, fitting, and designing letters—ever.

Interviewer: What kind of future do you foresee for publishing?

Godine: The number of people who care about books, who care about words, is declining. Publishers are professional optimists. They work in a shrinking market and it has been shrinking for five years. It's a problem of education. I think the education in this country is at the point of breaking down, or at least not fulfilling the kind of rational expectation placed upon it in the past. The home and the society no longer regard basic literary values as important. They were very important during the immigrant waves of the 1890s through the 1920s when every Jew and Italian and Irish kid learned to read and write because it was like a gift. Today, becoming educated is looked on as a chore.

Interviewer: What kind of future do you foresee for the Godine Press? Can you imagine your list changing significantly?

Godine: Each list is so different it's hard to say. We publish many illustrated and expensive books so I hope the economy holds up. I think things in this country are going to get worse and then they're going to get better. I think they're going to get better in late 1982, both the economy and publishing, and Reagan will have something to do with that.

    As for our future, I'm really excited about a book we're doing now by William Eisman for which William Gass has written the text. It's going to be dynamite. It's an adventurous book designed like a house and is virtually unreadable: it's printed in modules of 13, with a reflecting milar centre-piece, and has to be tipped over just to get to the text. It's going to be a very difficult book to bring off, and I hope to keep the price down to $15 or $20. We'll do it by printing 10,000, and floating it initially on the reputation of Gass, and on the fact that it will really be an interesting object as a book.

— Eric Burns

James Laughlin

New
Directions

James Laughlin of New Directions

This fall, *New Directions 43* will appear. In 1936, the first of these annuals included poets named Williams, Pound, Moore, Stein, Stevens and Cummings—none of them yet the cynosures of English departments. It also published the very new: three early poems by Elizabeth Bishop and a short story by Henry Miller, whose *Tropic of Cancer* had appeared only two years earlier in Paris. At the time, the 22-year-old editor-publisher, James Laughlin, loaded his Buick with 600 unpaginated copies, became a traveling salesman and persuaded bookstores to stock a few volumes—out of pity, he believes.

Laughlin, now in his 67th year, continues to reside in Norfolk, Conn., near the cow barn from which he started publication. In 1981 ND's New York editors and staff handle much of the work of publication, and W.W. Norton distributes more efficiently than the publisher had from his automobile. The annual's pressrun has escalated to 2,500 copies: 1,000 hard and 1,500 soft. The one-man rule of past years has devolved to consensus, but in a sense Laughlin has always collaborated: He has listened well.

Publishing Ezra Pound, he listened to Ezra Pound—which brought him not only William Carlos Williams but Henry Miller. Listening to Henry Miller, he reprinted Hermann Hesse's *Siddhartha*, which sold as many as a quarter of a million copies a year late in the 60's. Pound's friend Mr. Eliot recommended Djuna Barnes, whose *Nightwood* has been continuously available. Edith Sitwell recommended Dylan Thomas, and Dylan Thomas Vernon Watkins. William Carlos Williams recommended Nathanael West—as well as many terrible poets, especially from New Jersey, whom he would praise extravagantly, ending his letter, "but as you think best." Laughlin's Harvard connections—he was a sophomore when he first published a New Directions book—supplied him well. Harry Levin, who wrote his *James Joyce* for ND when he was in his 20's, supplied Vladimir Nabokov, and Albert Guerard John Hawkes—one of the younger writers Laughlin is proudest of. Laughlin met Tennessee Williams at a cocktail party—his only literary discovery with a social origin. He found Delmore Schwartz in the *Partisan Review* and wrote him a letter: Schwartz brought him Randall Jarrell and John Berryman. Laughlin cannot remember how he came across Kenneth Rexroth, who led him to Denise Levertov, Robert Duncan, Gary Snyder, Gregory Corso, Lawrence Ferlinghetti, David Antin and Jerome Rothenberg.

Although New Directions started in the service of verbal revolution, it reprinted Henry James, E.M. Forster, Ronald Firbank and Evelyn Waugh when other publishers would not; when no one would print F. Scott Fitzgerald's *The Crack Up*, ND did; when *The Great Gatsby* was out of print, New Directions brought it back. For the most part the list represented the new, with Objectivists George Oppen, Carl Rakosi, Charles Reznikoff; with Robert Creely, Michael McClure, Robert Duncan, William Everson; with Laughlin's particular friend Thomas Merton; with novelists James Purdy, Coleman Dowell, Frederick Busch and Walter Abish (who recently received PEN's 1981 William Faulkner Award).

Two glues held the list together: the assumption of quality and the assumption that these books would not sell in the marketplace. In bringing foreign authors to American readers in translation, ND may have made its most important contribution: not only the obvious Rimbaud, Baudelaire, Rilke, Valery, Kafka and Cocteau, but the less known and the unknown: Montale, Neruda, Queneau, Cardenal, Lorca, Pasternak, Paz, Borges, Mishima, Lihn, Vittorini, Parra, Guillevic.

Because such publishing required subsidy at the start, ND's story begins with a 19th-century immigrant. Laughlin's great-grandfather James Laughlin—the first syllable sounds like the Scots "Loch"— understood that there was a shortage of crockery in the New World. He sold his farm in northern Ireland, bought crockery, shipped it to Philadelphia, filled a wagon with it and started west. By the time he arrived at Fort Duquesne (later Pittsburgh) his wagon was empty and his pockets full. A devout Presbyterian, he founded a bank and a store and before he died joined forces with a Welsh iron-puddler to smelt iron. The patriarch's five sons entered the firm (Laughlin's grandfather James II became the treasurer) and made their fortunes—providing eventual support for books by Henry Miller and William Carlos Williams.

When James Laughlin IV was a boy in Pittsburgh, his father (named Henry; an uncle was James III) took the children down to the mill once a year at Thanksgiving. "It was scary—tremendous slabs of hot molten steel coming out of those giant furnaces, terrible noise, huge cranes carrying metal over your head all molten. [Although] there was never in my time any grim things such as the time when my great-uncle Frick turned the macheguns on the workers [during the Homestead Massacre], at an early age I made up my mind that I would not go into the mill."

Boyhood on the Hill, where the rich people lived, was pleasant enough, but Laughlin's life seems to have begun when he left Pittsburgh for Choate; he never came back to stay. Teaching at Choate was the poet Dudley Fitts, who had corresponded for years with Ezra Pound and later introduced Laughlin to the master craftsman. With the tutelage of Fitts and Carey Briggs, Laughlin found the purpose of his life. He edited the Choate literary magazine, wrote fiction, and published a prize-winning story in the *Atlantic Monthly* before he arrived at Harvard.

At least as important as Choate in the long run was the alternative home provided in Norfolk, Conn., by his father's older sister, Aunt Leila Laughlin Carlisle, who had bought 600 acres in Norfolk and built herself Robin Hill in 1929. He started visiting Aunt Leila in Norfolk from Choate; he has not left Norfolk since. A town of enormous white wooden houses, it is a northwestern Connecticut enclave of the rich. If you turn right on Mountain Road and go through two crossroads, after a half mile you come to the large white Meadow House of James and Ann Laughlin: set back from the road, with black-green shutters, surrounded by rocky pasture with white birch growing in it, sheep and a sheep barn. The land is hilly, hemlock over the granite fields, vistas north and west into hills of western Massachusetts and northeastern New York.

When Laughlin translated himself from Choate to Harvard, he continued to take his vacations in Norfolk at Aunt Leila's, who was powerful, childless, loving, dominant ("she should have been a man running a steel mill") and eccentric. Through a medium she communicated with a spirit named Lester who wrote long letters. Years later, when she worried over the books her nephew published, Lester would reassure her, saying not to worry about James, James is going to straighten out, be patient, he is a good boy. "Oh," says Laughlin now, "She was a wonderful old woman."

Aunt Leila was literary, with the taste of her generation—Scott, Thackeray—and could not countenance ND's list. By contemporary standards, of course, ND published no dirty books—and it was Aunt Leila who was chiefly responsible. As Nabokov's first American publisher, Laughlin could have taken a chance on *Lolita*—but counseled Nabokov to publish it first in Paris. As Henry Miller's publisher, ND issued books energetic but inoffensive—*The Cosmological Eye* (the cover illustration is a photograph of Laughlin's eye), *The Wisdom of the Heart, The Colossus of Maroussi*; 15 titles still in print—and Barney Rosset's Grove Press published the "Tropics" when censorship diminished in America. Laughlin admires Rosset's enterprise; but "I knew that my aunt would come down on me like a sledgehammer."

At Harvard Laughlin heeled the *Advocate* in his freshman year, made the editorial board and "hung around a lot." James Agee was a senior that year, precocious, writing the poems of his first volume. "I was in awe of him," Laughlin says. Later Robert Fitzgerald "began putting me onto the classics." Laughlin majored in the unusual combination of Latin and Italian, the Italian coming from his adventures on leave as a sophomore.

Despite the *Advocate*, Harvard in general was stuffy; it was a known fact that the Boylston Professor of Rhetoric and Oratory, the poet Robert Hillyer, would leave the room if someone mentioned T.S. Eliot or Ezra Pound. So Laughlin applied for leave—he became a pioneer of the multiyear B.A., taking his degree in 1939 at the age of 25—and went to Paris, where he consorted with Gertrude Stein and Alice B. Toklas; he was found useful for changing tires. Then he wrote Ezra Pound in Rapallo, presuming upon the Fitts connection, hoping to visit—and received a wire in return: "Visibility high."

Laughlin attended the Ezuversity in Rapallo for six months, studying Italian with an old lady Pound procured for him, Signorina Canessa—"about a hundred, stooped over like a barrel-hoop"—and studying everything else with the Ezuversity's sole professor. Tuition was free, books were loaned, examination took place over meals, or whenever the master paused in his labors. Italian lessons continued in the evening at the cinema, where Pound relaxed after his day's work, feet propped on the balcony rail, in a cowboy hat and a velvet coat, eating peanuts and roaring with laughter at bad indigenous comedies.

When Laughlin showed Pound poems and stories he was working on, Pound cut and cut and cut. Finally, as Laughlin tells it,

Pound suggested that instead of becoming a writer he should make himself useful to others by becoming a publisher. Never has advice been better followed.

It should be said, however, that Laughlin has continued to write poems in the interstices of his publishing career. Lawrence Ferlinghetti's City Lights published *In Another Country* in 1978, Laughlin's poems 1935-1975 selected by Robert Fitzgerald—a short book, the poems mostly brief, the accomplishments modest but solid: observations, notes, poems of love and tenderness. Normally easy-going in speech, Laughlin becomes tersely self-deprecating when he speaks of his writing: "It's very light; it's sentimental, it deals with no great subjects, no great thoughts...." Perhaps, if the poet pretends that he does not take his work seriously, he is free to continue it.

Coming back to Harvard from Italy, Laughlin founded ND with his own money. When he started college his father gave him $100,000, which he invested and which sustained him until the 50's, when he began to inherit more substantial sums. During the first 20 Years of ND, Laughlin acquired the reputation of a skinflint. When he hired assistants he paid low wages; when the cupboard was bare he delayed royalty payments. "Like other rich men patronizing the arts," says an old friend, "he makes a point of playing the hard-boiled pro rather than the dilettantish easy mark." But even the assistants he underpaid were witnesses to generosity. He published and promoted Delmore Schwartz, hired him to help edit, and later— when Schwartz in his paranoia attacked Laughlin to everyone who would listen, claiming that Laughlin collaborated with Nelson Rockefeller to cuckold him—paid Schwartz's psychiatrist behind Schwartz's back. "He had been so sweet, so funny! He just got loopy. I wanted to see if anybody could fix him up." When Kenneth Patchen and his wife were broke, Laughlin installed them in the cottage at Norfolk, attached to the end of the offices, where they would work and write and survive. (One time, when Laughlin was away skiing, Aunt Leila discovered that the Patchens were dumping refuse in the woods behind the cottage. "She blew her top and they were gone.")

In later years, when John Hawkes needed time away from teaching to work on a novel, Laughlin made him interest-free loans. "Thanks to him," Hawkes says, "I was able to spend essential years writing in Europe and the West Indies." But the money was not the most important thing to Hawkes: 'The main thing was his support, his steadfast encouragement in the face of vitriolic reviews or no reviews at all, the constant strength he lent me when fiction writing, or my kind of it, seemed nearly impossible." The books remained and still remain in print. For the most part Laughlin has done little line-editing for his writers, because they would not stand for it. "Henry Miller would not let you change a word. Bill Williams didn't want to change a line."

Not all relationships with writers were easy. Readers of Edmund Wilson's letters to Vladimir Nabokov will remember Wilson's continual hostility toward Laughlin. Perhaps the most difficult of all writers was Edward Dahlberg, who was once discovered in the ND offices ripping bookjackets from the walls, enraged because his own were unrepresented.

In the 40's ND began to issue books in series. Volumes called "Five Young American Poets" appeared for three years, providing the first lengthy publication of Jarrell, Berryman, Karl Shapiro, Tennessee Williams, Paul Goodman, Jean Garrigue, John Frederick Nims and Eve Merriam. "The Poet of the Month," 12 pamphlets available for $4.50 a year, ran for 42 issues from 1941 to 1944. (When the Book-of-the-Month Club threatened a lawsuit, the series became "Poets of the Year.") The series began with William Carlos Williams, followed by F.T. Prince, Delmore Schwartz, Josephine Miles, Robert Penn Warren, Richmond Lattimore, John Wheelwright, Richard Eberhart, John Berryman, Vladimir Nabokov, and Yvor Winters, among others.

There was also the New Classics series of reprints—Waugh, Fitzgerald, Forster, Stein, etc.—and the critical Makers of Modern Literature, which sponsored Trilling on Forster, Levin on Joyce, and Winters on Robinson. In the old annuals are notices of the ones that got away—books planned and never done. If only one could read those "forthcoming books" advertised in the 1941 annual. Henry James by R.P. Blackmur, Franz Kafka by Harry Levin, Baudelaire by Allen Tate, T.S. Eliot by Delmore Schwartz, and Emily Dickinson by John Crowe Ransom. Critical books actually published include John Crowe Ransom's *The New Criticism*, Yvor Winters's *Maule's Curse*, and William Empson's *Seven Types of Ambiguity*.

In one memorable summer of the 40's Vladimir Nabokov and family spent time with Laughlin at Alta, Utah, where the novelist-lepidopterist pursued butterflies and moths. Nabokov's fiction has never been praised for its compassion; he was singleminded if nothing else. One evening at dusk he returned from his day's excursion saying that during hot pursuit over Bear Gulch he had heard someone groaning most piteously down by the stream. "Did you stop?" Laughlin asked him. "No, I had to get the butterfly." The next day the corpse of an aged prospector was discovered in what has been renamed, in Nabokov's honor, Dead Man's Gulch.

Laughlin did some assistant-butterflying. "We nearly got killed once. At the end of the range there is a mountain called Lone Peak, about 13,000 feet high. He had the idea that at the top of this mountain there would be a certain very rare butterfly that would live only a day or two. We set off to try and get it. We drove at first by car through a canyon and then climbed up through the damndest jungle, about eight hours of climbing. . . . and there sure enough on the top was this butterfly!

"But we had made the mistake of going in summer clothes, in shorts and sneakers. As we started down this snowfield below the peak, we lost our footing and began to slide. We were sliding faster and faster down this snowfield, toward a terrible bunch of rocks, but Nabokov had his butterfly net. . . . He managed somehow to hook his butterfly net onto a piece of rock that was sticking through the snow. I grabbed his foot and held onto him. Then he crawled back to the rock, and somehow figured out a way. . . . If it hadn't been for that butterfly net. . . . "

There are a thousand stories. With Dylan Thomas there was a three-day London binge which ended when the two men, with several unidentified companions, woke on the floor of a female stranger's flat. With Thomas there was also the desperate loan of a hundred pounds, on the ground that his eldest son had been committed to a tuberculosis sanitarium, an event elsewhere unrecorded. With Elizabeth Bishop there was a polite tea party at a Key West brothel called The Square Roof, of which Bishop had befriended the proprietor and her employees.

Many publishers have approached Laughlin for his memoirs, which will never be written. "When they ask ya to do yar meemoirs"—Laughlin imitates Pound—"ya know ya're finished." But the documents of ND, available to scholars, are protected in Norfolk in a fireproof room together with thousands of rare books and magazines. A resident archivist keeps them in order. Most of them will go to Harvard.

At this age Laughlin does not work so many hours as he once did. In winter he likes to crosscountry, in summer to play golf and swim in Toby Pond. And he does his own investing. Still, he reads manuscripts six or seven hours a day, usually until one or two in the morning. Still, he comes to New York once a week—Ann Laughlin drives the two and a half hours while her husband reads manuscripts beside her—staying overnight at their Bank Street apartment and working with the ND staff nearby on Eighth Avenue. When Laughlin worked for the Ford Foundation in the 50's, editing the international magazine *Perspectives* among other things, Robert MacGregor handled the bulk of ND work. MacGregor died four years ago. Now Frederick Martin heads a staff of seven, and manuscripts are accepted by discussion and consensus.

Beginning with the sales of *Siddhartha*; helped by the million-copy sale of Lawrence Ferlinghetti's *Coney Island of the Mind*; by the academic acceptance of Pound, Williams, and other old authors; by the amazing sales of younger poets like Gary Snyder and Denise Levertov; and by the growing backlist sales of John Hawkes and other discoveries, the firm has been in the black for two decades. In some of these years, however, the black was thin.

Laughlin could sell ND if he wished, but he does not choose to. (Only recently a rich friend offered to buy the firm for his child, who had just graduated summa cum laude and was interested in publishing.) Instead, planning for a future without the publisher, Laughlin has set up a trust fund to insure that ND will survive his death for at least a decade—time, as he supposes, for his authors to find other publishers. If they succeed, most will need to find publishers that resemble ND, which will not be easy. These are publishers of the middle way—larger than the one-owner small press, smaller than dinosaurs ponderously sustained by Big Books only—who by low overhead, by infusions of capital from the responsible rich, by wit, or most likely by all three—can choose with taste, publish with economy and keep a good book in print.

— **Donald Hall**

John Martin

BLACK
SPARROW
PRESS

A Happy Publisher

John Martin is a lucky man. His publishing firm, Black Sparrow Press, succeeds at selling books of poetry, fiction and literary nonfiction (and *only* these). At a time when the larger New York publishing houses are "cutting back" to a few token volumes of poetry and "literary fiction" each year, Black Sparrow continues to specialize in literature.

Like many small publishers, John Martin operates out of his home, a villa in the north end of Santa Barbara. Behind his house is a separate building, roughly 14 by 12 feet, which was originally a pool house. Here he has his Black Sparrow office, his Addressograph machine, two typewriters and his postage stamps. (Metered postage is not his style.) The glass walls of his office look out at the Santa Barbara mountains, and in the back yard, 20 feet away, is a fair-sized swimming pool. New York publishing was never like this.

A tall, trim, bald and bespectacled man, born in 1930 in San Francisco, Mr. Martin grew up in Los Angeles, discovering literature as a teen-ager. One reason he dropped out of the University of California in Los Angeles during his first year was that his favorite modern authors—Ezra Pound, D.H. Lawrence and Wallace Stevens, among others—were not then taught.

Instead of college, he went to work in an office supply store, beginning as a factotum. Within three months he was managing the place. A dozen years later the company had grown from three employees to 40. Since he had access to printing machinery, Mr. Martin issued five broadsides of the poetry of Charles Bukowski, a Los Angeles writer who extends and exceeds Henry Miller in his vivid portrayal of low life; and Mr. Martin gave them freely to the secretaries and clerks in his office supply company. (These broadsides are now worth several hundred dollars apiece.)

As a hobby Mr. Martin collected first editions of the modern masters, which he found in used bookstores mostly around Los Angeles. "Instead of smoking," he reminisced in distinctly California tones, "I spent 20 years' cigarette money scouring for first editions." By the 1960's, luckily for Mr. Martin, the libraries of new and expanding universities wanted first editions they did not have. He sold the collection in 1965 for $50,000; he kept $35,000 for himself after commissions and taxes. With this money he started Black Sparrow, quitting his job and intending to live off his publishing until his bank account ran dry. Unlike so many American literary publishers who based their firms on inherited wealth, Mr. Martin had no money other than his own; and to this day his only assets are his car, his house, his library and his publishing business.

The first full-length books he did were Ron Loewinsohn's *L'Autre* (1967) and Robert Kelly's *Finding the Measure* (1968). Before long, the several hundred copies of each title sold out, "giving me enough money to pay off the printer and make a few hundred dollars. I discovered I could make a living doing this kind of thing." Since his favorite modern poets were Stevens and Pound, he thought that at first he would concentrate on "their legitimate descendants," as he now calls them, and so published writers associated with the Black Mountain school of American poetry—Robert Creeley, Robert Duncan, Fielding Dawson and Paul Blackburn—as well as personal favorites like Bukowski and Diane Wakoski. "All the authors I really liked, who were productive and living, would give me all their work, or if they had contracts elsewhere, were delighted to give me some of it." He paused and added, "All these people I'm pleased to have discovered on my own. No professor told me."

From the perspective of 1980, he can see that his business "turned around" in 1970. That was the year of his nadir, "when I had $100 in the bank account and thought to myself, this is it, I'll have to get a job." A second, different crisis came in 1973, when he published D.H. Lawrence's *The Escaped Cock*, which is the original, unexpurgated edition of a text previously published as *The Man Who Died* (1929). Before publication Black Sparrow had orders for 2,000 books—far more copies of a single title than he had ever sold before—and so for the first time he hired someone else, a young shipping clerk. "Until then I did everything myself—shipping, receiving, bookkeeping, invoicing, production management, dealing with authors. I did everything except book design, which my wife Barbara did, and some editorial work that Seamus Cooney, a friend in the academic world, did. I worked 80 hours a week, out of a small Los Angeles apartment."

Meanwhile, Mr. Martin had been collecting first editions, manuscripts and other literary materials of D.H. Lawrence; and in 1975 he sold this collection to the University of Tulsa library for a check large enough to become the down payment on the current Santa Barbara nest.

Black Sparrow's books are stored on neat shelves in the Martin basement. He is his own stockboy, personally filling orders that are meticulously mailed with newspaper wrapping and cardboard backing from a shipping table in his garage. Each working day, to his backyard office come a full-time assistant, a part-time shipping clerk and a part-time bookkeeper. Currently, Black Sparrow each year ships 150,000 books, grosses around $500,000, pays its authors over $75,000 in royalties, publishes 15 new titles, and rewards its owner with $20,000 income. To this day he has never incorporated, because, he explains, "I do business as myself, not as a corporation."

One way that the firm has recently changed is that it is now publishing more fiction than before (if not more fiction than poetry) and more literary nonfiction as well. Among its books for mid-1980 are Henry Miller's notes on D.H. Lawrence's novel *Aaron's Rod*, Ekbert Fass's book-length critical essay on the poet Ted Hughes, a novel by John Fante, and two volumes of the complete correspondence of the Black Mountain poets Robert Creeley and Charles Olson. Having once published books in editions of less than a thousand, he now issues at least 2,500 copies; and his best seller for 1979, Charles Bukowski's *Women*, sold 25,000 copies.

In characterizing his company, Mr. Martin uses the term "independent publisher" to distinguish it not only from the commercial publishing houses, but from those that are economically dependent upon literary grants. *Independent* means to him that he is "independent of market, of pressure groups, of literary establishments and granting agencies, and of the authors themselves. I can literally publish what I like. Since I am a totally literary person, I have no desire to publish anything in any other area. I want to die never having been to Las Vegas, gone to Disneyland or watched a whole TV show, except for sports."

One reason he moved from Los Angeles to Santa Barbara was that his initial printer was there, Mackintosh and Young; and this printer remains a keystone in Santa Barbara independent publishing.

Upstairs from the print shop, on Santa Barbara's magnificent State Street, are the offices of Noel Young's Capra Press, which specializes in literary and "life-style" books; Ross-Erikson, which does literature and Eastern mysticism; and Mudborn Press, which does poetry, fiction and autobiography. Nearby in Santa Barbara are other successful publishers who also specialize: Woodbridge in food books; Pat Bragg in health books; Parachuting in books on aviation and self-publishing; Turkey in poetry and art; and ABC-Clio in scholarly art books.

However, even among his peers, John Martin is special. As Noel Young put it, "He disregards the procedures of publishing, or what they are supposed to be; and I don't know how he gets away with it. He doesn't advertise; he doesn't apply for grants or get loans; he pays his bills on time; he doesn't call meetings of his salesmen; he doesn't go to book fairs or booksellers' conventions; he doesn't do commercial books to support his literary titles; he doesn't go to parties that authors or bookstores arrange for his books." In many ways, Black Sparrow establishes an enviable standard.

Judyl Mudfoot of Mudborn Press says, "Our whole view of publishing is different because of John. His example makes surviving and succeeding as a literary publisher possible. I would view it entirely differently if I never met John." Even outside Santa Barbara, many small poetry publishers are imitating Black Sparrow, not only in the design of their books, but in their manner of operation, although none as yet is commercially successful.

True to his image of himself as scrupulously independent, Mr. Martin has conducted his business in isolation. Remarkably few of his writers have met him more than once, and some have never met him at all. Even though he has so far published nine of Joyce Carol Oates's books, for instance, the two have never met. "That means," he explains, "I keep my attention on their work, rather than on their personalities." He reached behind him for his latest Oates title. "She has given me, in my opinion, her best work. Bless her." He kissed his fist.

The business of Black Sparrow has settled down. There are on hand hundreds of "standing orders" from libraries, taking hardback editions of every Black Sparrow book; and he will soon celebrate his own achievement by publishing a bibliography of the first 300 titles. Having let his earlier, thin periodical *Sparrow* die, he is presently founding a new, thicker literary journal entitled *Blast*, after an earlier magazine published by Wyndham Lewis (his current literary hero); and he promises, "It will be the most important literary journal of the eighties. It will be mean—and lean."

Glancing from time to time at the distracting mountain view outside, he calculated, "At bottom every successful publisher has an altruistic love of literature, but as businessmen they let commercial considerations override their personal taste. I've had at least 10 or 15 commercial publishers tell me that they wish they could do what I do. Whereas I get a high out of every book I publish, their satisfactions are fewer and farther between. I get 15 highs a year, while they get only one every two years."

— Richard Kostelanetz

James Boyer May

TRACE
A VILLIERS PUBLICATION

An Influence on the Language: An Interview with James Boyer May

James Boyer May grew up in Wisconsin, where he attended Lawrence University and Beloit College. His first appearance in print was with a poem in the *Milwaukee Journal* in 1924, for which he was paid ten dollars. When he was twenty, and serving on the *Marinette Eagle* (Wisc.) he was the youngest city editor in the United States. Later, he was one of the country's more prolific poets. In 1952, he initiated *Trace* magazine and, within it, introduced the Chronicle, a directory of little magazines that has helped to cross-pollinate the writer's craft throughout the world. In the late fifties, Los Angeles poets and audiences enjoyed the public readings that he conducted and his radio program on KUSC FM, USC's station. He was also an editor of *Poetry Los Angeles*, an anthology. Now, at sixty-six, he is terminating *Trace* with a big double issue 72/73, largely because of considerations of health, but he will remain on the board of directors of Villiers Publications, Ltd., the British-based publisher of *Trace*, and he will assist Len Fulton, publisher of *The International Directory Of Little Magazines and Small Presses*. He is also turning once more to his own writing and poetry. He makes his home in Los Angeles with his wife (known to readers as staff member G.E. Evancheck) who helped him through discouraging moments over the years.

Interviewer: *Trace* came out 3 times a year then, or was it quarterly?

May: Originally my schedule called for three a year. Then I went to five with a vacation through the winter seasons, you see. In other words, every two months, except the winter months I skipped four.

Interviewer: That's kind of a heavy schedule...

May: Then I went quarterly—I think it was about 1960. So that by numbers, now for the *year*-period it works out about right—73 numbers in slightly over eighteen years. So that, divided by four, it seems like it was quarterly.

Interviewer: One reason that I was interested in you professionally is that you must be the premier, the granddaddy of them all, because a good many of the publications last only a few months or a year, two years, from what I've been able to gather.

May: You'd be surprised. I've worked out the averages several times. What the exact current thing would be I don't know but only about seven or eight years ago I did a statistical study based upon all the magazines then listed in my directory and found that the average length of life of a little mag was about eleven years. And I did a statistical thing on the slick magazines that you get on the stands and they had a much shorter life span than the average little magazine so I don't know how this fiction came about. There *are* so many of them that start and stop and of course it's true that there are a great many of them that just come out with one issue and quit.

Interviewer: I thought, because, you know most people who write poetry—a lot of them—are apt to be college students (this is where we seem to be getting some of the best work so far) and if you're going to write poetry particularly it's apt (I would imagine) to start hitting you between seventeen and through the undergraduate years in college. When the young fellow gets out and he starts raising a family and gets into all this it may be frowned upon, as a consequence—and I would suppose that the people who edit are comparatively younger, usually.

May: A good percentage of these people, though, are teachers—they become teachers—as a result of which they do stay with it, and this has to do with the life span of a great many magazines. A fellow may have been an undergrad as an editor of a magazine then he later gets his Ph.D. and teaches somewhere, succeeds in persuading the school wherever he is to give him some support and his magazine continues. I could think of instances—Guy Owen is now quite a well-known writer, you know, and a movie was made from one of his novels[1], it was a very successful movie (he's one of the people, by the way, that I first published, too, years ago). Well, Guy has had little magazines, you see, from years back. So the address changes as he goes from school to school. It's the same editor, you see.

Interviewer: When did you start *Trace*?

May: It was '52 in June. But this was not a deliberately conspired thing at all. I had been doing this column, "Towards Print" for *Matrix* which I think started in 1949 and they were the ones that persuaded me to do this because they knew that I had a very large correspondence (don't ask me how this came about, but it did) after I got out of the army.

Interviewer: *Matrix* was a quarterly?

May: Yes. And *that* lasted quite a good many years. I think it was founded along about the late thirties and it lasted until '52. At different times they had several well-known people on their editorial board. They were the first publishers of Anais Nin, for instance. They published a couple of her things way back in the thirties. But it finally came to the point where there were just two editors left and *Matrix* was coming out rather sporadically and at this point they moved here. They had been in New York and Philadelphia. They looked me up. They had the notion that since I was familiar with the field—the little mag field—that I should have a little directory and a feature editorial thing in each of their issues, so that was the beginning of that. At the same time I was working with Whipple McClay, who had the *Gallery*, which was a bibliographical thing on the little mags. He had a heart attack in the spring of '52 and died and the editors of *Matrix* decided to quit. So that was the way it got started— it was just a place to continue the work I'd been doing, that's all.

Interviewer: So it sort of involved the directory...

May: The directory—and of course I did run some little articles. Cid Corman[2] had an article in, I think, my second or third issue—various people—of course long before this I had this thing of correspondence. And I corresponded (*did*, until later years when I haven't had time) with writers in all parts of the world.

Interviewer: Was this a sort of personal correspondence?

May: Yes, and it was due to this, you see, that I was able to get lines on where these different publications were because I knew people in Australia, New Zealand, South Africa, Europe, Asia—I had friends in Japan, India, South America. And that was how I got my information about little mags. Then, naturally, when I got the name of a little mag I'd contact the editor and he'd be on my *roll*. But apparently nobody other than Whipple McClay had actually started to do bibliographical work in this field.

Interviewer: In the first issues, along with the directory, did you start to run short stories?

May: Oh, no. *Trace* was called a "Bridge" by various people—and it *was*—between people in many parts of the world—but it was fundamentally the directory and the written content consisted pretty much of my own comments on the various periodicals. I did a book[3] on the little magazines at that time which was pretty much of a follow-up on that one from Princeton University Press[4]. During this period there were a great many letters published—these letters were largely from editors of little magazines explaining their aims and purposes and then there'd be arguments amongst them and it was kind of a forum for the little magazine people. The immediate result was that you'd see American and Canadian writers published in an Australian magazine and Australian writers published in England and so on all because of *Trace*—because *Trace* went to these different people and they saw these different periodicals and they sent their manuscripts where they otherwise wouldn't have sent them.

Interviewer: Cross-pollenization.

May: Right. It's my belief, and I think it could be documented, that we had an influence on the language itself. If you have a thousand little mags—suppose they only have a circulation of two or three hundred—still that's quite a few, because they're in different areas and different people are reading them so they do get a spread that way. To me, anyway, there was a great deal more difference in the way the Scot poets, for instance, were writing, than the Canadians and certainly as between the United States and Australia. You could almost pick a thing up and say "this is like a foreign language—they have a different way of expressing themselves." So they influenced one another and I think this had an influence on English.

May

Interviewer: Sounds most helpful and very pragmatic.

May: And it was a lot of fun. And I think it was along about 1960 that some people said, well, you know, you sound forth with your opinions of what's good and what's bad—why not have some examples of this? So then I decided to enlarge it and put in a section of original writings and almost right away I also started publishing art. I've also been able to help a good many artists and photographers.

Interviewer: Yes, I've liked some of the collages. But generally, the art in the literary or small magazines seems kind of discordant sometimes. Some of the photography I don't care for—it seems eclectic to me. But yours, in most cases, of what little I've seen—I've only seen three issues—contemporary issues—I've liked very much.

May: Well I've been accused of not running any editorial line because I've published virtually every kind and type of writing and the reason for this is that I don't hold to any clique or special sort of slant as to what a poem should be or what a story should be. I try to understand on the basis of a background of general reading what a given writer is trying to do in his own way, you see. Then, my judgement on it is not based on the kind or type of writing it is but how well I think he does what *he's* trying to do. So the result of this is that I sometimes get accused of publishing a hodgepodge because there are so many different kinds and types of things there.

Interviewer: I don't know—perhaps that's the best way to go about it. Just getting into the field now, I have the impression that there is a tendency to have Bloomsbury Schools or cliques, or something, you know.

May: Oh, yes.

Interviewer: And I'm going to try to avoid that myself—I don't know whether I *can*!

May: This is quite generally true. There are some excellent periodicals—some of the finest—in which the editor has a very special idea of the kind and type of thing he wants to publish, but he's still doing a good job. *Kayak* is an example of that. It's an excellent periodical but narrow. He has his particular idea of what he wants and this is *it*. I could read a poem and tell whether (George) Hitchcock would publish it or not. And that's not a judgement on the poem—I'm judging it on the basis of what I know about what Hitchcock likes. So I wouldn't say this is always bad but oftentimes it is bad because you have a "schoolish group" and they have some cranky notion, you know—either you should have articles or you shouldn't have articles or too many verbs or you shouldn't have any adjectives in poetry and I think these things are rather silly.

Interviewer: *Lit Scene* is going to be—hopefully—a sort of general conveyor of a comparatively high profile and it will be referring back, in its pages, to other mags—like I'm carrying trade news from all over. I'm going to be fairly broadly-based even in the suburbs—in shopping center bookstores—so I imagine I'll be less specific and more generalized but I'll be pointing *back* to these other publications in its pages.... What was the trend in the fifties, when you were first starting out, was there more prose being published, or more poetry? I believe that William J. Margolis was telling me that even in the fifties, when he started out himself, there was a balance heavily in terms of poetry as opposed to fiction. Has it changed much?

May: No. Good original fiction is quite hard to come by. I mean, speaking as an editor. The general quality level, however, of poetry is very bad, very bad. I'm talking about manuscripts coming in. I did a little breakdown on this last year and at that time I was accepting far less than one half of one percent of the stuff that was coming in.

Interviewer: Are they really that bad or are you extremely....

May: They're pretty bad, really. Most of it's pretty bad.

Interviewer: Where does it seem to come from, college students?

May: No, no. At a casual estimate I'm sure there are hundreds of thousands of people in this country who are trying to write poetry and they range all the way from high school kids—I have published not a few high school kids, by the way—good, bright kids—and I also discovered that I had published a couple of octogenarians who were very bright, you know. Some people don't age that way. And these are housewives, they're old maids—I mean they're all kinds and types of people—and some of the old maids aren't too bad, you know, some of them are pretty good.

May

Interviewer: I suppose a good many of them have been published before in other publications or they wouldn't keep on?

May: No. The average of these—they're very dogged—they'll go on and on and on for years and years without an acceptance. Someone whose work I took a couple of years ago wrote me and said they had been submitting manuscripts to editors for twelve years and this was their first acceptance. I have also, besides seeking—or favoring, what shall we say—new people—I have published the work of some people who were quite well established some years ago but fell into disfavor because of personal enmities or radical political involvements. In my estimation, you see, this has nothing to do with anything. If they do good work, I don't care *what* they are, you know. So I have brought back, I guess, a few people who were in disfavor—hadn't been published much elsewhere for years although they had been very prominent. One of those is Walter Lowenfels who now is being published widely, but you know he had a long period there when he wasn't. Well, what led to this—Robert Lowry, you see, in the forties—

Interviewer: Is this the Robert Lowry I'm thinking about—*Through the Panama?*

May: He wrote *The Cage* and so on—*The Wolf That Fed Us*—very famous writer.

Interviewer: Maybe I'm confusing him with the *Ultramarine* and the other....

May: No, that's the other one—

Interviewer: *Malcolm* Lowry.

May: Yeah. But critics were writing about him in the late forties as one of the two or three greatest living novelists and all this sort of thing and then just—cooled—he started to go through a period when he began to have exaggerated notions about being ill-treated and he antagonized some people prominent in the publishing world. He wrote some wild things and so forth and he just—fell out. And for this reason—*not* for that reason—but for the reason that I liked his work I published some of his things some time ago and I don't know that it has helped him too much but at any rate it's helped him psychologically. He had this one story—and of course I didn't know this at the time—the manuscripts that he sent me were always beaten all to hell because he was circulating them and getting them rejected all over the place—I took this one story and he wrote me about it. This was a story that he had originally written in the forties and hadn't really done anything with it. And then he started sending it out—and he told me how many—I think it was well over one hundred rejections.

Interviewer: Oh, my gosh. Persistent fellow—

May: On this one story, you see. Well, you asked me how persistent people are. Well, here was this famous writer who was just in a bad way because of special circumstances. But he was determined that he wanted to get this story published. I thought it was a good story. So did our readers.

Interviewer: Well it sounds like you've done well with at least *one person* if you've done this—you've fulfilled, I would almost say, your mission as an editor. Any other writers stand out from those early days of *Trace*?

May: Well, there are so many different ones. [Goes to bookshelves.] The really old ones I have downstairs. One of the things I was doing—I'd sort of forgotten because I haven't been doing much of it lately—is getting interviews. I'd get somebody to do the interview, so we had a few of these.

Interviewer: That's a good idea, I think.

May: You know, there are so many names here I wouldn't know where to start.

Interviewer: Oh, that's quite all right. Were there more literary magazines being published at that time—eighteen years ago, 1952-3? Who were publishing them—returning veterans?

May: No, *this* has been a period of terrific increase in these publications. I did a—it was 1968, I guess it was—I think I had the statistics there.

Interviewer: You had an article in one of the very recent ones—about

May

the undergounds and some of the trends.

May: Now that I'm quitting I'm writing some editorials giving the story of it. The number of magazines has just multiplied like crazy. Through the fifties and sixties these magazines have multiplied—not only individuals starting magazines but more and more schools have—of course oftentimes this is a matter of the school wanting a certain prestige—they feel it's prestigious to have a little magazine, you see.

Interviewer: Not realizing the hell and headaches they're getting into.

May: Well, they can afford it. The trouble is of course that it's thinning out. The quality has deteriorated, naturally, because of the fact that there are so many outlets.

Interviewer: Why the increase suddenly now? What do you attribute it to?

May: I attribute it to the Establishment. Reaction against centralization and control and all this sort of thing. It's a desire for independence, I mean an independent expression of personality and so on and so forth. Of course, that's the operating principle behind *Trace* as far as that's concerned. That's what I want to encourage. People don't want to be mass—what shall we, say, you know? And you can't *find* outlets. The book publishing business is in a horrible state now, as a result of this. It's been deteriorating ever since the twenties and it's getting very bad. In other words, the way they figure, there has to be a ready-made market, you see. A mass market. So actually *if* they are, the little mags have been—they'll be credited, with having saved our culture because otherwise it would become stereotyped. The average commercial magazine publisher has to hit a mass audience to survive.

Interviewer: For the advertising.

May: Right. So these—no matter how *good* the work—if it's too different and would not be understood or would be rejected by a great many people, of course, they won't publish it. James Joyce would have had a hell of a time getting published. Well—there are the little magazines—some little magazine would have taken him up.

Interviewer: Of course—even Berkeley ten years ago—1959—I was around the area then and I loved to go in the bookstores there—it was just when the paperbacks were really taking their stride, you know, and of course *that* seemed to me like a great specialization right there. And of course it *was*, I suppose—many titles and so forth. It's an interesting phenonomen. Because I was wondering if there were more now, or less. Being such a neophyte I had no idea.

May: They've multiplied terrifically. There are more today than there have ever been by far. City Lights—Ferlinghetti, of course—has done a great service for this field—breaking the barrier to sales of poetry books. These many, many poetry books that he's put out—he *proved* that there was an audience for poetry, you see. There was a long period of time from roughly about the time of Longfellow 'till the fifties when people—I mean, there was no interest in poetry—they *said* there was no interest in poetry—but you see, there really *was*, only it just wasn't getting out. And City Lights did this—they put these things out and sold editions up to a hundred thousand copies. They're still doing it.

Interviewer: How did they promote?

May: Well, he built up his own, apparently, pretty much. A big percentage of his sales was through his own store there in San Francisco. And then they tried different distributors and they have their own distribution unit in England—they sell a great number of books in England.

Interviewer: I think distribution would be the greatest problem.

May: It is.

Interviewer: Because, here I live in Long Beach and where am I going to go to pick up little magazines? Sometimes Lordan's has some, but I have to go all the way, many times, into the Free Press bookstores. Twenty-eight *miles!*[5]

May: I gave up on that type of distribution years and years ago. (May goes on to contemplate the woes of dealing with retail outlets and distributors, the loss of time it seemed to involve, for him, and of cases where bookstores were tardy or failed to pay.)

Interviewer: How *have* you distributed? College bookstores? Private subscriptions?

May: Private subscriptions. You see, I was lucky in the beginning—I got a little write-up in the *New York Times Book Review* on the very first issue which brought me one hundred and eighty-seven subscribers right there. And that was a good start, you know. Then of course I had the small subscription list I had inherited from *Matrix*—they turned all of their stuff over to me. And after that it was a very, very slow uphill climb to achieve any kind of circulation because the falling off—the number of people who don't renew—is not too much different from the new subscribers coming on, you see. So that's where the problem is.

Interviewer: Where would you get most of your subscribers, in starting a magazine—do you essentially write college libraries and so forth?

May: Well, I built up the libraries very slowly, too. In the beginning, I think, with the first issue only twenty or thirty libraries, then sixty and seventy and so on, and now today there are roughly four hundred. They're mostly college or university libraries.

Interviewer: How else would one promote? I'm indicating this not only for myself but for other people who may be wanting to start something.

May: Well, that's the big rub in this sort of thing. Your advertising differential is tremendous. That is, suppose you're running an ad in the *LA Times*, you're paying, in other words, to address one in a thousand... I tried advertising in the *Saturday Review, Village Voice*, various publications like that and the ads never paid for themselves— I'd get a few subscribers. The best ad I ever got, I mean as far as returns, was an ad in a theater lobby thing.

Interviewer: Here, locally?

May: No, it was a national thing. It went to—I don't know how many theaters. They'd pass it out in the lobby, I guess... And that's the best return I ever got, but you see this type of theater— these people would also be interested in new writings, you see, so that probably accounts for it. But other than that, little mag people help each other by exchanging their subscriber lists. I obtained years ago the list of *Western Review*,[6] which was quite well established and had a circulation of about thirteen hundred, and from theirs I got some—in other words, direct mail to subscriber lists of other little mags or literary quarterlies. I'd say that's the best source.

Interviewer: Did you advertise on an exchange basis in any of the other magazines?

May: I've never found that it paid—I don't know whether it paid the other end—it didn't pay for *me*, so I haven't had many of those—

Interviewer: You don't trade out then?

May: Well, I have. See, here's *Arts in Society*—I've traded with them for a time, and maybe I got a half-dozen subscribers from it, I don't know.

Interviewer: Speaking of that (the fifties) period, how were the Beat writers as a group compared with the Hip writers of today? It's a very hard distinction to make, I guess. Were the Beats writing very much? Ginsberg came out of it and Jack Kerouac was involved with it.

May: Well, I've written several articles about this. It's a little complicated. In the first place, it's wrong to make a classification of this kind, because these are all individuals and they're all different and you can't just say well, so-and-so is a Beat writer—in other words, you have to speak specifically about a certain individual and certain writings. In other words, it's arbitrary categorization I'd say. As I say, I've written several articles about this. I had an article in *Adam*[7] on the subject.

Interviewer: Would you say, essentially, though, that the "Hip" if we can call them that—the San Francisco movement—the psychedelic movement—it seems to me that this was more *visually* oriented rather than typographically.

May: Well, to what extent this has real literary relevance, it's hard to say at this point. A lot of the publicity, the publicity attendant on *Howl* and so on, really had nothing to do with literature—it was strictly news-chat, you know, and the results were that a lot of things got published but for irrelevant reasons. The reasons for the publication had nothing to do with literary merit or anything else, you know, it just had to do with the fact that somebody had a lot of publicity.

Interviewer: Promotion.

May: Yeah, right.

Interviewer: It's a little unfortunate, I guess.

May: Yeah, well, I don't know—it could be *good*, you never know.

Interviewer: How have you organized *Trace* in recent years—I mean, how is the staff arranged and how do you tackle manuscripts, in other words?

May: There was a time—it's quite some years ago, now, when we tried to get together editorially and somehow it didn't work out. I tried to save it from being one of these lowest common denominator things by saying that if any one person liked something well enough—even if all of the others were against it, we'd publish it. That's one way of keeping—you know, a board-is *bored*! (Editorial Advisor) Gil Orlovitz has been in New York for years—many years since he's been here. He's made some very valuable general suggestions about the conduct of the magazine from time to time—he's found some writers for me there, you see, and has sent on to me things and has given me names of people. But of the people that have actually been *here*—it came clear quite a long time ago that it would be a physical impossibility for me to read all of these incoming manuscripts so I devised a plan whereby at least one, and preferably two, and sometimes it was possible for three—to go over these manuscripts and I would only read the ones that they would pass on to me. And we did that for the last five or six years.

Interviewer: Would you like to mention some of their names?

May: Milton Van Sickle, Alexandra Garrett, Robin Johnson, Warren Netz, Netz has helped me a *lot*. and Helen Luster, G.E. Evancheck and Gerald Sobral, A. Frederic Franklyn (who handles Film) and John V. Sankey (European Editorial Associate and founder of Villiers Publications). In years past there was Curtis Zahn, Lawrence Spingarn . . . Zahn's quite a well-known writer now and so is Spingarn, who has had many publications. And then of course, one of the most published writers in the country was at one time one of my associates—Guy Daniels, the Russian translator. There have been many different people. The fact of the matter is, you see, that the course of *Trace* has been decided pretty much by the people that *get* it. In other words I feel that there are a couple of hundred or more people who have had an influence on the course of *Trace*.

Interviewer: This brings me to another point. Do the desires—and tastes—of your readers seem to synchronize with your writers and the sort of material that they write? How do you think the relationship between the little mags and their readers and writers compare with magazines of larger circulation? Are the readers and writers of *Trace* closer—

May: Well, apparently so because I've had any number of letters over the years—by the way, one of my policies has been never to publish a letter praising *Trace*—I never publish letters of praise or anything like that, but there have been thousands of them. I have quite a few prominent subscribers—people who are internationally known and famous. I could, if I wanted to *use* their names, tell you about some of these people who have written to me that they consider *Trace* the best magazine in print. And writing to me that "I let my subscription to the *Saturday Review* lapse—*Trace* fills my need." Things like that, you know, which is nice—makes me feel good. But I shouldn't say that about—*Saturday Review* is one of my subscribers—I better be careful! Of course, it's all over now!

Interviewer: What's the future for the little magazine? You're getting out of it now—and I'm kind of sorry to see you leave—I'm just getting acquainted with the field and I see some of the people like yourself leave and it makes me wonder what the future is for these things.

May: Well, I think that the future is tied to the individuals who will carry on. There are a great many of them and these are vigorous, and, shall I say, strong people so I think it will go on, sure. The reason I'm quitting, of course, has to do with my health. I don't bear up well under strain any longer, you know. . . . It's partly a matter of personalities—in fact, personalities have a lot to do with it. You see, for instance, at the time when there was Franklyn, Spingarn, Zahn, and myself—and we are four individuals—we clashed all the time. It was very bad, oh yes! (laughs)

May

Interviewer: Now, did you see each other regularly, or was this through the distance, through the phone?

May: No. This was when we'd get together, you know, and try to go over the manuscripts and we'd have some horrible fights.

Interviewer: Orlovitz was in New York, then, himself?

May: Well, at one time he was also here. Orlovitz and I always hit it off pretty well—I mean, our opinions and so on pretty much coincided. But there's a nervous strain here, in contending with someone, you know. And of course, I *did* make the final decisions, anyway, but I just decided it would be better to do it the other way. That is, in other words, people read the manuscripts and they don't discuss it and if they feel it's *something*, my instruction always has been—if it's different, or in any way they feel that it has literary merit—to pass it on.

Interviewer: And of course this (the original manuscripts) would come through the post office box here and—who would pick up the mail? You'd—

May: Oh, I always pick up the mail and they'd come over here. Usually one at a time—sometimes two or three. But we rather studiously avoided verbal exchanges over these things!

Interviewer: It's far more difficult, isn't it, than if you were running, say, a conventional trade magazine on modern dental care or something, because that's comparatively neutralized but this is something that's getting into something that's very difficult.

May: Yes.

Interviewer: Do you think that the kind of society we're apparently moving through—we were just mentioning that the mass media is under fire now, by being part of the Establishment—with the development of specialized life styles—of course, that's all coming into its own, now.

May: And there are others. But the Life Style thing—this is "the thing." It's becoming more and more difficult to find yourself and this, of course, is the great problem of our time—the individual—or

I may say the lost individual.

Interviewer: It's a chronic disease as far as that's concerned.

May: Sure. If you just look at tv and the daily papers and the magazines from the newsstand and see what you see on the street and so on and so forth—you'll never discover yourself that way—you can't. . . .

Interviewer: It's quite a situation—the break up of the empire, shall we say. Maybe little magazines will lead us—

May: Well, they're a counter-influence. And in *Twigs as Varied Bent* I pointed out the relationship—the more highly industrialized and advanced a country is the more little mags you'll find. There's a definite ratio there. I made a breakdown and the highest percentage —*this* is not based on the number of mags but the number of mags related to the population—on that basis the United States led the world. England second.

Interviewer: I've had a feeling about England, particularly.

May: Canada—all these industrially advanced countries, you see— Germany, and so on. And then you get into the less advanced countries and you don't find any little mags. They don't need 'em, you see, because they're still living. It's in the big countries where people are dead. And they have to have things like this.

Interviewer: You divide it into terms of living and dead—in other words, in the smaller countries you're alive to possibilities and you don't need it.

May: Right, right. You really can live your life, you know, but in a mass society you're just a cog.

Interviewer: What's the solution then (for) a happy human society— is it to bust the United States up into a—biodegradable smaller unit, or what?

May: Well, I don't know.

Interviewer: Would the ideal situation be to have less little magazines and happier people?

May: I theorized once that if the world could be broken up into, say, several hundred thousand little countries maybe we could prevent war.

Interviewer: I've heard of this.

May: Right. And (with) so many people, you see. Now Carl Linder's been helping me recently and he's a film man you know—he just won second prize, by the way, up in San Francisco in the erotic film festival.

Interviewer: Is he a filmmaker-director?

May: He's a filmmaker. He makes these after midnight things, you know. He's quite famous, quite well-known in that field. He also is a good writer—I'm publishing a piece of an unpublished novel of his in my final issue . . . But Carl had been talking about this and this also has to do with what you might call the rebellion in the film industry. All these little filmmakers. Because they can't be individuals at a big studio—it's the power-mower—and if they really want to do an individual piece of work it's like a man writing a novel—he has to do it *himself*, you see.

Interviewer: Of course, in terms of filmmaking you have to have a certain amount of capital behind you to make a feature-length, I guess.

May: Well, it isn't so horribly expensive as you might imagine, and it's not too hard to get backers, either, if you have any reputation. People put up money for you to make a film, you know, if they have confidence in you and so on. There's a pretty good distribution of these things. Carl's getting his royalties all the time—his films are shown all over the United States and Europe. *Evergreen* has a film distribution.

Interviewer: Who was it—Sir Herbert Read, the English art historian —or artist— (and social & lit critic) was saying that—

May: He's one of my great favorites. He died just recently.

Interviewer: —And he was comparing—discussing the ideal city—of size—either a nation or of a city-state and he was referring, I think, back to the civilizations like Greece where you have—there's a certain balance of the population and you get *beyond* that and art and everything else suffers.

May: Oh, yes.

Interviewer: It's hard to respond to it.

May: Right. But the artists, too, are finding a way. Actually there's a terrific production of art of all types in this country today. The mass of people are not aware of it at all. But it's here, Seymour Gresser, one of my contributors, that's one of his things there (refers to a large piece of sculpture in the room). He's become quite famous as a sculptor and sells his pieces for enormous prices. But there's a great deal of overlappage. I mean we find a very high percentage of writers also paint—and great many painters also write and sculpt, and so on and some of them do many things.

Interviewer: Is this more true now than it was in the past?

May: I think it is and I think that's part of it—I mean it's part of the individual rebellion.

Interviewer: What are your critical feelings about the younger poets and writers of today? Are you enthusiastic about the multi-media concept—light shows and poetry readings combined, and that type of thing? I feel we're getting more into the visual, non-linear—

May: Well, I was involved with that in the late fifties and assisted in putting on a great many things—music and poetry and things on the screen and all this sort of thing. I did it myself, in fact and I did readings to music and that was when it was—Patchen really was the innovator there and he was the one that first came on with all this. He's a very good close friend of mine.

Interviewer: How is he now? I mean, he's been unwell. (Patchen has suffered for many years with a spinal ailment.)

May: Very bad—he's in bad shape, terrible.[8] But, anyway, my feeling about this is that this is something else. I mean if it's successful to the extent that it pleases a great many people and so on and so forth—that's fine—but I really don't think it has anything to do with literature, let's put it that way. You see what I mean. No, I mean that it's a "thing." OK, so it's good. So why worry about it.

Interviewer: It's not something to build a critique around, in other words.

May: There has to be, in the final analysis—if this is going to stand or fall—I mean if it's a piece of writing it's going to stand or fall on its literary merits and that's it. . . .

Interviewer: There's a tendency to blend—Charles Bukowski was mentioning it (in the Dec. '70 interview)—he said that Steve Richmond and he were writing poetry on boards to get people to read the stuff.

May: Yes. We also have many poems that, when read—particularly read by a certain person—are very effective, and you see them on a page and you wonder why. I mean, really. That's what I mean by "it's another thing," you know. I have all sorts of poetry records over there (on the shelves) and at least a whole closetful of tapes of poets that I had here—people used to come here from all over the world and I told you I made twenty-seven or twenty-eight recordings of poets for the Library of Congress. But the point is that the oral thing is really a separate thing, I'm convinced of that.

Interviewer: I think so, too.

May: It's like a song, I mean, and it depends upon the singer. And it *can* be a very poor piece of literature.

Interviewer: I think I'll be attending some poetry readings, I suppose, but I think fundamentally my role—of course I'll be accepting news from the workshops—but I think most of my work's going to be done behind the desk. At least initially, because I'd rather not get into personalities myself and I'd rather—it's easier, it's probably less difficult for me to *read* the poetry at my leisure than. . . .

May: Right, right. No—you're absolutely right about this—you can wear yourself all out. That's one of the reasons I gradually got out of this because it's quite a nervous strain, you know, and oftentimes you have to be hypocritical, or feel that you have to be and say nice things and you really—think it's a lot of junk, you know. So I've sort of gotten away from it—as you say, behind a desk—that's the only place.

Interviewer: Well, as you say, it takes up an awful lot of....

May: It takes up time. It's also a bad thing, oftentimes, to personally know a writer. Some of them are very disagreeable characters, really. And their writing, on the other hand, may be great, but they're real bastards. I mean, really! You wouldn't want to be involved with 'em.... Then you can be influenced the other way, adversely—I mean adversely for you as an editor because some of these people are so nice and so pleasant and so on and so forth and their stuff just isn't really all that good but if you know them personally they may convince you to publish something you'd be sorry you published. Because they're so ingratiating. So, you see it works both ways. So it's better *not* to make personal contact with these people.

Interviewer: People may get mad at me for not, you know—although this doesn't *preclude* personal meetings.

May: No, no...You see, many more people I saw before I started publishing original poetry and fiction. When I said that people came in from all over the world and I made these tapes and so on—this was all before I started publishing the stuff. Once I'd started publishing things—of course this was not entirely intentional—my wife became very seriously ill and we just couldn't have anybody over here and so that sort of cut it off and ever since that we've never resumed soirees of that kind, you know. So that was the way it worked out—it was for the best, of course.

Interviewer: What, in your opinion kept *Trace* going for so many years while other magazines and publishers fell by the wayside?

May: Well, I don't know. I guess I was just willing to spend a lot of money! (his heartiest laugh in an amiable conversation). I need it! I *need* it!

Interviewer: What traits do you think were involved in the success of *Trace*? In other words—putting it another way—what complaints would you have with publishers of little mags today? Why do some little magazines *fail*. Of course, there are probably as many reasons as there are magazines.

May: Right.

Interviewer: Just assume you're talking to someone just starting out—well, you're talking to *me*, of course.

May: Well, I believe in the ferment. So I would never discourage anybody from starting a magazine because who knows what will come, you know? It's all part of the ferment. If they have the urge, and the ambition and the vigor and so on—let 'em go to it.

Interviewer: Anything that he or she should watch out for or any pitfalls—obvious pitfalls that he's apt to fall into that so many may have in the past? Spending too much, initially—or things that relate to editorship—or lack of editing?

May: Well, usually they overdo it. The smaller the scale they can start at the better their chances, or course. And a great many magazines have failed because they blew the whole thing, you might say, on their first issue or so, expecting what didn't happen, because it's a very slow process of building up a magazine. *Trace* started out very modestly—very modestly—with sixteen pages.

Interviewer: I kind of went overboard then—fifty-three pages 8½ by 11.

May: Oh, well, that's not so bad.

Interviewer: I didn't intend to—I'm cutting back to about 35.

May: And then that'll build up and get gradually bigger and bigger. Of course the losses kept getting a little bigger all the time but at any rate I didn't just go broke in the first, you know. But other than that I think the main thing to watch out for is excessive self-interest.

Interviewer: Explain. Explain a little more.

May: Well, an ego is a fine thing, you know. You have to have it. But many magazines seem to have gone down because their editors wanted to—what shall we say—they were eager-beavers. In other words, they wanted to—make something that would make them big, you know—and it didn't work.

Interviewer: I see. So they were more oriented toward their own needs rather than—

May: Right, right. In other words this personality or life style and so on is all well and good, but the editor must realize that he's living in a world of other people and to give consideration, you see, to others—Intolerance has characterized many of the little mag editors who have had to fold.

Interviewer: You mean in terms of selecting other manuscripts?

May: Well, they become irate—someone disagrees with their publication and so on and then they'll devote pages of argument justifying themselves and all this sort of stuff, which can be very bad.

Interviewer: Because the readers's not too enthused about that.

May: No! No,—the editor thinks that he's a genius and wants the world to know it and this sort of thing, you know. And maybe he *is* a genius but he'd better be a little more quiet about it.

Interviewer: Well, I think you've done a very *good* job. Is there anything you'd do differently if you were starting *Trace* today?

May: I really don't know that I would—but looking back I can see that I sometimes expanded a little too fast, and I didn't mark up my sales price fast enough.

Interviewer: You didn't progressively keep the thing going?

May: No. I could have had a higher per copy price and a better subscription price and not have lost so much money. Things like that. . .I think from a practical point of view I would have up-priced the magazine. Now whether I'd have slowed down my expansion I don't know, because there was a great deal of what I thought was very fine material and I wanted to give it print.

Interviewer: Is distribution any easier through organizations like COSMEP?[9]

May 97

May: They're working at it. I don't know what kind of results they're getting, I really don't. But with an organization maybe it's possible, maybe they can really do something about this thing.

Interviewer: Make the bookstores pay, for example.

May: Yes. I had a letter from somebody in New England. I can't remember who it was[10]—but any bookstores in New England that owed me some money, why he was writing to all the book publishers and magazines and asking them and he was personally going to take a trip around through New England and all these bookstores and collect the bills. That was kind of nice, wasn't it?

Interviewer: Yes. Did he succeed?

May: No—I mean just a couple of days ago I got this letter—that was an interesting project—a personal project, I guess.

Interviewer: Just getting down to some biographical data—when and where were you born—are you native Californian or English?

May: Oh, no. Of course that's all in the books—

Interviewer: I know you're sixty-six.

May: Yes. I was born in Wisconsin and my father went to school in England so that's how I happened to get over there, as a small child. But that has no bearing on anything, I'm sure.

Interviewer: What was your education—college here, in the states?

May: I went to Lawrence College—it's now Lawrence University in Wisconsin. I had a little scholarship and I went there the first year and then I went to Beloit College, which is also in Wisconsin—you know where it is, down on the Illinois line.

Interviewer: Any desire to write show up at an early age? What was the forerunner of all this?

May: Well, I was first published in 1924. I got ten dollars for a poem.

Interviewer: Not bad. . . .

May: It was the *Milwaukee Journal*. On their editorial page and they had a little illustration for it.

Interviewer: What writers did you admire when you were young, and has this changed?

May: I don't know, really. I had access to—my father had a large library. Read from the time I was just a little kid.

Interviewer: I think this is very important, and I think a lot of kids who are underprivileged—ghetto kids—they just don't have the backing behind them.

May: No. They don't. So that's all accidental—I mean, it just so happened.

Interviewer: You were engaged in publishing since then?

May: I had intentions of staying with journalism but I decided it wasn't good because you get into a stereotype. You have to write fast and you have to write every day and it gets so a certain situation—I had a terrible time breaking away from that after years on the newspaper.

Interviewer: What newspapers were you on?

May: Well, when I was twenty I was the youngest city editor in the United States on a daily newspaper. That was the *Marinette* (Wis.) *Eagle Star*. They had a circulation of 5,000.

Interviewer: That was kind of young.

May: Yes. . .I had kicked over the traces and left school the year before. Marinette is an old city. At one time it was bigger than Chicago. Really! It's at the *upper* Lake Michigan there and has a fine harbor. But Chicago did far outstrip it, didn't it?

Interviewer: What were some of the other papers you worked on?

May: *Rockford Morning Times*. (In Illinois, outside of Chicago.) No

May longer exists. *Oshkosh Northwestern*...I've done a lot of publishing. At one time, before the coming of *Trace*—as of 1952 I *believe* I was the most published poet. I don't know—it must have been fifty or sixty things in print all over the world.

Interviewer: Fifty or sixty books or individual pieces?

May: No, just individual pieces of mine you know, scattered all over. But *Trace* came to take up more and more of my time and now I think I'd like to go back and try to get this stuff organized. I was pretty indiscriminate, you know, on it—stuff just published all over and this was before the days of *Trace*. Of course the Second World War kind of messed me up—I got involved in that.

Interviewer: In the Army?

May: In the Army, yeah. I was in there for the duration. And of course my literary prospects didn't prosper...Well, I made up my mind even before *Trace* started that there were so many people writing and so on that I was never able to—what shall I say—really sell myself on my own stuff to the extent that I felt that it was just that great. And it seemed to me—and gradually it became a conviction— that it was a much more important thing for me to do what I did with *Trace* in helping all these other writers and so on, than it would have been had I concentrated my energies on my own writing— because who is to know—as I say, I just didn't feel my own writing was all that great. And I felt that from the standpoint of cultural service, or whatever you want to call it, that this was the better thing to do. I've had an opportunity to actually influence, to some extent, the course of literary history through my editorials and with what I've published in *Trace*, an influence which I think was considerably greater than it would have been just to have published my own writings... You see, I've had other things in mind, too, in connection with *Trace* and that is that it has a fairly international circulation. I feel that this—and things like it—are influences toward peace, because if the people of one country get to know enough about the culture of the people of the other country they're less likely to fight.

Interviewer: Ignorance is not bliss, in this case—it's very volatile. I'm looking very closely for addresses right now—utilizing your directory for mailing out and soliciting information.

May: Good.

Interviewer: Which continent now seems to be coming on in terms of literary interest. India? Does that seem to be? Or Africa?

May: Well, there's so much trouble in Africa. There was this very good *Transition* magazine, published in Uganda and this poor editor had his place demolished, I mean they just went in and destroyed all of his records and everything, threw him in jail. He had a trial and was acquitted but under their law you can be held six months after you're acquitted. Isn't that crazy? He's in Paris, now, and hasn't been able to get started up again. It was a very fine publication. But things are pretty rough in Africa—not conducive to this sort of thing.

There's a lot of literary revolt going on in India at this time—young people—the hungries. . . .

Interviewer: Hungry for basic lack of food or ideas?

May: Both, I guess. No, these are just the poor young there. They've brought out some very interesting material. A great deal of their writing, of course, is in English because for years and years their schools were English. And I've made some good contacts there.

Interviewer: South America—what's the situation south of the border?

May: South of the border is very hot. Yes—it is! Yeah, there's a lot of wild stuff going on down there. I get a lot of their magazines. They're mostly in Spanish and I don't read Spanish too well, but I get the drift.

Interviewer: Are they kind of opening up?

May: Oh, yes, yes. There's a lot of activity down there—a lot of activity. It's also surprising how conservative countries—you'd think of Australia and New Zealand as being conservative countries, but some of the little magazine stuff that I've been getting from there is *wild*.

Interviewer: . . . It's good cause for optimism, I think.

May: Well, yes—it shows that we're alive. The world is alive.

— **William Robson**

[1]*The Flim-Flam Man* released in 1967 by 20th Century Fox (from the novel *The Ballad of The Flim-Flam Man*) Macmillan Co. 1965. Owen's recent project has been *Southern Poetry Review.*

[2]Cid Corman is a well-known poet with several books in print. He has revived his magazine *Origin* and does much critical writing.

[3]*Twigs As Varied Bent*, by James B. May, pub. 1954 by Sparrow Magazine, New York City, as Vagrom Chapbook No. 1.

[4]*The Little Magazine*, by Frederick J. Hoffman, Charles Allen, and Carolyn F. Ulrich. Princeton Univ. Press, 1946. (Allen is now introducing another book.)

[5]The Editor has also discovered the Agoric Black Market Bookstore at 4700 E. 7th St. Long Beach—and found a great repository of underground and little mags. Lordan's is at 4818 E. 2nd St. (Belmont Shore) in his home town.

[6]This magazine was originally *Intermountain*, Utah. It became *Rocky Mountain Review*, then moved to Iowa City as *Western Review.*

[7]"The Original Underground," by James B. May, *Adam* Feb. 70.

[8]The *Mt. Alverno Review*, "A Quick Anthology of West Coast Verse," a single, has recently been released and all proceeds will go to the Patchen surgery fund, reports Editor Michael C. Ford. Features Patchen, J.B. May, Jim Morrison (The Doors), Bukowski, David Ossman (of Firesign Theatre) and others. $3.00 per copy at Free Press bookstores, or send to Michael C. Ford, Box 5143, Ocean Park Station, Ca. 90405.

[9]Committee of Small Magazine Editors and Publishers. May, along with Felix Pollak, chief of the Special Collections Library at the U. of Wisconsin, is an Advisor to **COSMEP.**

[10]Gerard Dombrowski of **Abyss Publications.**

Barney Rosset

Grove Press, Inc.

Barney Rosset, the Force Behind Grove Press

It is not unusual for Barney Rosset to dream that he is an aerialist. In these dreams, the spotlight is on him and his attire is clearly meant for flying through the air. There's just one problem: he does not know the first thing about *being* an aerialist.

As the trapeze swings toward him, he reasons with dream-like logic, "This is obviously what I am, so I must know what to do." Without any idea of how he'll keep from crashing to the ground, he always grabs the trapeze. At that point, with Rosset confident that another element will somehow surface and be responsible for his survival, the dream always ends.

For the past 27 years, that is pretty much the way it has been for Barney Rosset and Grove Press, the publishing house built around his highly developed instincts.

At first, it was a one-man operation with not many more titles, financed by a million dollar-plus legacy from Barent Lee Rosset Sr., a Chicago banker. After 10 years of skating on the edge of bankruptcy—a state exacerbated by Rosset's involvement in the landmark obscenity trials that gave us *Lady Chatterley's Lover* and *Tropic of Cancer*, and freed writers to consider sex—Grove blossomed into *the* publishing house of the '60s, flush with dramatically new ideas, interests and profits.

For a number of reasons, some of them exceedingly curious, Grove has shrunk back to an eight-person business. Now, when publishing houses are more easily associated with corporations than individuals, it is only slightly theatrical to call Rosset the last independent publisher in New York.

"Who else is there?" an editor from a corporate subsidiary wonders rhetorically. "There's Barney and there's Farrar, Straus and Giroux."

Because Grove reflects Rosset's personality to such an extent, the two of them are impossible to separate.

The FBI, the CIA and the Army, whose records include a somewhat baffling chart of Rosset's existence, would probably agree. According to the Rockefeller Commission report, Grove was the only private enterprise to be unduly harrassed by intelligence agencies. In Rosset's office, three large cabinet drawers are filled to capacity with files obtained through the Freedom of Information Act. The data goes back to his days as a student at Chicago's progressive Francis W. Parker School, which the 57-year-old Rosset describes as "a bigger influence on me than my parents or college."

It is safe to assume that the parents of Rosset's Irish Catholic mother did not push her into the arms of his Jewish father, who lost his first million at an early age and made up for it several times over. He was their only child.

In a description pertinent to Rosset's subsequent career as a publisher, one of his Parker teachers wrote that, "being a spoiled boy . . . he does nothing he doesn't want to do." Both his shyness and boldness are duly noted. Furthermore, his "brilliance, energy and powers of leadership" ought to be carefully guided, since he had the potential for becoming "an outstanding facist or a fair, sensitive, democratic leader."

Concern for young Barney's potential facism no doubt arose from an earlier interview: "Application for registration in the Parker High School made by Subject when he was 12 years old stated that Benito Mussolini was the living person most admired by Subject." In the margin, Rosset has scribbled, "Remarkable! This keeps turning up. I would love to see that application."

Rosset, who can't remember ever admiring Mussolini, probably decided boring questions deserve outrageous answers. He's also on the record stating his life's ambition to be "a loafer." Rosset has always made room for the bright, naughty boy in himself. And, as a consequence, so has Grove.

At a time when every publisher in America was conscious of the criminal sentences dealt to bookdealers who sold *An American Tragedy*, Rosset was remarkable for insisting that D.H. Lawrence's *Lady Chatterley's Lover* was literature, not smutty filth, and therefore deserved First Amendment protection. The process began when the Postmaster General refused to mail cartons of the book; it ended with a 1959 Federal Courts decision in Grove's favor.

None of the above prevented hundreds of local communitites from taking booksellers to court in an attempt to stop Grove's edition of Henry Miller's long-banned *Tropic of Cancer*. Rosset first determined to publish that book when, as a sophomore at Swarthmore, he bought a contraband copy in New York so that he could write a paper, which he presciently titled, "Henry Miller vs. Our Way of Life."

Definition of Obscenity

Rosset footed the bill for 60 separate state and local prosecutions brought against *Tropic of Cancer*, and for six state supreme court rulings (New York, Florida and Illinois found it obscene, Wisconsin, California and Massachusetts did not). The issue was finally resolved in the book's favor by a 1964 U.S. Supreme Court Hearing.

From those cases, a new definition of obscenity based on social importance eventually emerged. To argue them, Rosset hired Charles Rembar, a young literary attorney with whom he played tennis at his East Hampton home.

"Barney is a very unorthodox tennis player," says Rembar, whose analysis of Rosset's game could be a metaphoric description. "He uses both hands, but not at once. He's very quick and has enormous speed and endurance. Playing as doubles partners, we've always been able to beat players who are actually better than we are."

According to Rembar, *Lady Chatterley*, Grove's first bestseller, was a more difficult case to win than *Tropic of Cancer*. "There was a much greater bias," he says, "against books that made sex look too good."

Legal issues aside, at a time when an entirely new generation of writers was ripe for a publisher to call its own, Rosset made Grove theirs. Of course, other American publishers could have printed Samuel Beckett (Grove published *Waiting for Godot* two years before the play came to Broadway), Robbe-Grillet and Jean Genet; or brought William Burroughs' *Naked Lunch* out of censorship-imposed exile. But other publishers didn't understand.

In the early 1950s, Richard Seaver was in Paris publishing an English language literary magazine called *Merlin*. He met Rosset as a green publisher looking for writers.

"He very rightly understood that for a small publishing house to compete in a tough American market, Seaver says, "the approach would have to be different. He sensed or smelled or thought that there were European authors who, because of the war, were not published in America. And, as very often happens following a period of conflict, there was a burst of creative energy to be tapped."

In 1959, Seaver became managing editor of Grove, a position he held for 12 years because "Barney was the only other publisher with whom I felt a total affinity." Now, after establishing a Seaver imprint at Viking Press, Seaver is in charge of trade publication at Holt, Rinehart and Winston.

John Rechy, a Texan whose 1964 novel, *City of Light*, caused a sensation with its description of homosexual male hustling, says Rosset's outsider status figures largely in the books he has published.

"I consider myself an outsider, and I think Barney retains that quality, which puts him in touch with writers doing new and different things. Here's a man who's known and published some of the top writers of the century, for God's sake, and when I'm in New York, we go to some dive where the black customers make a big fuss over him. He's just drawn into a different milieu than most publishers."

Grenade Through the Window

Rosset may have been pointlessly protesting history when, at the age of 17, he picketed *Gone With the Wind* as a racist movie. But it helps explain why he later published LeRoi Jones and *The Autobiography of Malcolm X*. Once, in what appears to be classic Rosset style, he managed to offend both civil rights activists and opponents by printing what now seems to be simply a sensitive photograph of a white woman and a black child, both of whom are nude.

That photograph appeared in *Evergreen Review*, Grove's bimonthly cultural magazine—"a lewd little satellite in the publishing empire of Barney Rosset," in James J. Kilpatrick's description some years ago. In 1965, as an *Evergreen* cover featuring Che Guevara hit the streets, a band of Cuban exiles launched a grenade through a Grove Press window, an act Rosset regards (without substantiation) as one of the most successful CIA-directed anti-Castro missions.

Besides generating controversy, *Evergreen* harmonized perfectly with Grove's books, printing works by Jack Kerouac, Lawrence Ferlinghetti, Richard Brautigan, Pablo Neruda, Norman Mailer, Terry Southern, Jean Paul Sartre and Robert Coover, among others. Allen Ginsberg's *Howl* first reached a wide public through *Evergreen*

Review's second edition, which was devoted to "The San Francisco Renaissance."

When financial difficulties finally shut down *Evergreen* in 1973, it went out with the Rosset imprint. The last issue was devoted to *The Last Tango in Paris* and illustrated from a print pirated out of a Parisian moviehouse and delivered to Grove by an obliging stewardess.

Fred Jordan, a British-educated Viennese who recently left Grove after 23 years, was managing editor of the magazine and, like Seaver, remains a close friend of Rosset's. In his office at Grosset and Dunlap, where he is another one of publishing's handful of imprint editors, Jordan discusses Grove's past. "I hardly ever think about it nowadays," he says, "but the fact is, you can see me lighting up. I was a part of this. And for that, I'll be eternally grateful to Barney.

"Barney's genius was to be in tune with the tenor of the times in a totally un-selfconscious way. In projecting what he liked, he happened to be directly on target. It's so rare nowadays, not to look first at what the market wants, but to look primarily at what *I* want. It's an extraordinary conceit, really. Barney is still doing that—Grove is very much alive today. The times, however, are not as alive."

Rosset himself is not comfortable making what Jordan calls "these grandiose connections."

"You have to remember," Jordan warns, "in the beat generation, people made a fetish out of inarticulation. It's about *being* things—art is and people are."

For the past four years, both Rosset and Grove have operated out of a three-story, fortress-like townhouse on West Houston Street, where Rosset's living quarters are cleverly separated from office space. Since Grove began, neither the man or his business has ever been located north of 11th Street, south of Houston, east of Broadway or West of Seventh Avenue. Greenwich Village is crucial to the identities of both.

For some time now, Rosset has been surprising people who don't expect him to have a repertory of expressions that includes a shy, sweet smile. On this day, he has driven in from his East Hampton house, a highly elaborated quonset hut originally owned by the painter Robert Motherwell. Giving a whirlwind tour of his home, Rosset says, "My daughter (Tansey) is at camp, my son (Beckett) is in East Hampton and my wife (Christina, his third) left me."

Remains Friendly

Through his first wife, the highly-regarded painter, Joan Mitchell, Rosset not only came across a publishing house for sale; he also developed a fine eye for abstract expressionist art. But he never collected the work of the rising artists—like Willem De Kooning, Franz Kline and Jackson Pollack—who were friends and neighbors in East Hampton. Gifts on his walls include a Giacometti drawing from Samuel Beckett and several water colors from Henry Miller.

He remains friendly with his first wife, also a product of the Francis W. Parker School. Rosset's second wife, a German woman named Loly, is the mother of another son, Peter, and edits Grove's Eastern studies books. Her father, also a banker, was a German Intelligence officer during the war. From birth, it seems, Rosset has been integrating strange elements into his life.

"And I've kept track of them all," Rosset says, "believe me."

That is not difficult, especially when Rosset produces proof in the form of several different photograph albums, a rapid means of reminiscence perfectly suited to his temperament. Since Rosset headed a photographic unit in China during the war, that period is extensively recorded—in more ways than one, as the nearby files attest. Throughout his Army career, Rosset was suspected of "disaffection."

Why? For what was then fairly standard liberal stuff: his anti-war stance in high school, his sympathy for Spanish revolutionaries, his great admiration for the Soviet Union (which ended, never to be regained, with the Soviet-German non-aggression pact), his involvement at UCLA with a group of anti-Hitler "Jewish radicals." Most damning of all, apparently, was his correspondence with a girlfriend whose father was Japanese and whose mother was Caucasian.

Rosset's problems with communication are longstanding. Their letters, exchanged and recorded during his basic training in Corvalis, Oregon, had him suspected of being a Japanese espionage agent.

"One thing I'm unable to convince anyone of," Rosset says, "is that I was given the job of reporting on any subversive activities, fascist or communist, by enlisted men and officers in my outfit. I had to write a letter every week to a post office box in Portland. As there *were* no fascist or Communist activities, I invented them—but I only invented facist ones. I knew full well I wasn't getting anyone in trouble. But *I* was in trouble."

When Rosset learned that enlisted men could neither drink in local bars or socialize with University of Oregon coeds—rules that decimated two major interests—he quickly applied to Officers Candidate School. Once an officer in China, he hoped to meet Mao, a dream nurtured ever since he'd read Edgar Snow's *Red Star Over China*.

"Unfortunately," Rosset says, "I made the mistake of saying so to my superiors." This writer-of-letters-to-a-Japanese-girl was not allowed to take his camera either in or over Yanan, the communist capital. Flipping to a photograph of Mao taken by one of his men, Rosset says, "Grove now publishes *Red Star Over China*. That was kind of a badge of honor to me."

Later, Rosset would confuse his fans at the CIA and FBI by publishing in paperback a book called *The New Life*. The hardcover version, as it turns out, was published by a CIA-subsidized house. "I call that unfair competition," Rosset says. He is not kidding. That accusation is a pearl in the string of suits Rosset has filed against about a dozen officials, including Richard Helms, William Colby, and James Schlesinger.

"So far," says Rosset, "we've won the right to sue. And it's hopeless, you know. I don't want a money settlement, except to cover legal expenses (which the ACLU is helping to defray). I want an information settlement."

When this interview ends, it had progressed from awkward to comfortable. Tomorrow, Rosset is told, things should probably get more specific. "Oh," he says, "that's never as much fun."

The next day, Rosset is sipping on his morning glass of wine. Coffee was put off-limits to him a year ago, when a doctor looked at his x-rays and said, "You're dying." The diagnosis was bleeding ulcers. Considering Rosset's wiry, youthful appearance, they are the most obvious sign of a life lived largely on nerves. The news that he might be dying did not convince Rosset to submit to an operation. He wanted advice from "my doctor," an old Francis Parker friend in Chicago who apparently is to medicine what Rosset is to publishing.

Many of Rosset's publishing colleagues confine their admiration to his censorship battles. "People feel uneasy about Barney," Fred Jordan says, "like they feel uneasy about the '60s."

Certainly Rosset does not make things easier by doing such things as inviting two women who frequented a bar he knew of to join his party at a rather stuffy publishing banquet—a naughty way of allerting his associates as to whose company he found more stimulating. When people who know Rosset are asked to recount their favorite Barney Rosset stories, many of them, it turns out, are either unsuitable for a family newspaper or require elaborate background.

Rosset, by the way, never did allow that ulcer operation. As he might say, another element surfaced . . . and caused survival. Perhaps his confidence was high because Grove managed to survive the financial equivalent of bleeding ulcers.

In 1968, though, there were no warning pains. Grove had over 100 employes, four floors of office space at University Place, a 158-seat theater, a bar, an expensive I.B.M. computer for data processing, its own warehouse operation, several paperback lines, and a growing film division. Its biggest bestseller to date, psychiatrist Eric Berne's *Games People Play*, had been published.

The time seemed ripe for Rosset to revive his interest in films. In acquiring an extensive experimental film library, Rosset's most sensational and profitable purchase was a Swedish import called *I Am Curious Yellow*.

With profits from *Yellow*, Grove invested heavily in foreign films and a large building on Mercer Street. Of course, the film was controversial. In 1971, when Grove's ulcers were in full swing, the Supreme Court upheld a Maryland decision banning the film from that state.

"That is an interesting story," says Fred Jordan. "Maryland's case against *I Am Curious Yellow* was the first to reach a state supreme court. They held against us, and we appealed. At the time, Jerry Ford was minority leader of the House, and he was launching a drive to impeach Justice William O. Douglas. Barney and I were coming back from Denmark when we saw the Herald Tribune—Ford was on the cover waving a copy of *Evergreen Review*, saying that Douglas was writing for a pornographic magazine." (*Evergreen* had excerpted the last chapter from Douglas' book, *Points of Rebellion*.)

Douglas subsequently excused himself from all cases involving Grove—including the court's next case, *I Am Curious Yellow*. That ended in a tie vote, which had the effect of upholding the previous decision.

But then, Grove has demonstrated something of a knack for closing the door on itself. After opening up the sexual dialogue in literature, much of Grove's erotica (like *Story of O*, a French prostitute's account of sexual slavery) was crowded out and strippped of its mystery by totally artless porn. After Grove invested *I Am Curious Yellow* profits into avant-garde foreign films, that market promptly dwindled, thanks, in part, to the porno wave started by *I Am Curious Yellow* (a film that would scarcely merit an R-rating today.)

But before the Supreme Court had its say, angry women were standing outside the new Mercer Street building wearing buttons that read, "I Am Furious Yellow." Their protest was against Grove's "sado-masochistic literature and pornographic films that dehumanize and degrade women." Several women, one of whom had been employed by Grove, were arrested for occupying executive offices. Grove did not press charges. "The shame of it was that Grove would have been interested in publishing the sort of books they wanted," says Kent Carroll, now Rosset's top editor.

The Chaos Was Total

Simultaneously, the Fur, Leather and Machinist Workers was adding to the crush on the sidewalks in front of Grove; that old, leftist union was picketing in its attempt to make Grove its first publishing conquest. For months, Rosset says, "the chaos at Grove was total." Whether the union won or lost, he told the union, financial difficulties would force Rosset to fire a large number of employes. The union lost, and did not attempt to unionize another publishing house.

"We destroyed them," Rosset says, "and that was really painful to me. The demands we got were things like I had to abandon my house in East Hampton to a black women's collective, divide all the profits and put in a day care center. In the end, it was a disaster for everybody . . . I deeply believe the FBI and CIA backed it all, and that Grove's antiwar stance had something to do with it. I think that's one of the pieces I'm missing. But I don't think the head of the union, or some of the women, were aware of being duped."

The causes of Grove's financial problems were more direct. The recession hit just after Grove had borrowed heavily to finance its new building. No one wanted to lease Grove's expensive computer, which often sat in a costly idle state. Business was not good. The warehouse was oversupplied and had to be emptied. "At that point," Rosset says, "Random House got into the picture and offered to do our distribution."

While Rosset was not happy with some of the terms, it was a key to survival. Recently, Random House's involvement was reduced to what's called fulfillment—billing, shipping, warehousing and collecting. Grove is now handling its own sales. Rosset considers such an arrangement with a large concern like Random House—a subsidiary of RCA—the only chance for independent publishers.

"The government and a lot of people concerned with books think that conglomerate ownership of publishing is very bad," Rosset says. "I agree. But nobody says how things can be changed in a healthy way. If a company like Random House would deal with a little company like Grove, and make a profit from doing it, we, on the other hand, have financial and editorial independence. You could get small companies flourishing under the protection of big ones. It would be almost like a co-op.

"It's also a way to break up conglomerates. Anybody who believes there is no interference is either stupid, naive or lying. Among other things, Gulf and Western owns Paramount, Simon and Schuster, Pocket Books and a sugar plant in the Dominican Republic, which CBS recently did a documentary on. Now, if Paramount does a movie denouncing the operation of that plant, based on a book published in hardcover by Simon & Schuster and in paperback by Pocket Books, *then* I'll believe there's no interference."

Meanwhile, Random House really has no choice, since Grove still owes the company money for its inventory. Grove has made money the last four years, which is not bad. At a time when backlists are no longer a high publishing priority, Grove's still has an index of over 400 titles. The biggest problem Grove has in competing in the present book market is the high cost of buying material and promoting it.

Bookstore chains are another problem, since their buyers are inclined towards large printings and promotional budgets. "If you say 3,000 copies and you're waiting to see the reviews to tell if you're going to advertise at all," says Rosset, "forget it. That one—I don't know what to do about it."

For all of its associations with ideas and ideals, Grove remains a business, the most commercial aspect of which are its psychology books. "People shouldn't expect a publisher to have one solid line," Rosset says. "He has to be like an amoeba. There are certain things you can't do, and certain things you must do, but a number of other things in the middle."

One of those things that Rosset felt Grove must do was Gilbert Sorrentino's *Mulligan Stew*, a literary farce which, since its publication last June, is slowly gathering excellent reviews. Kent Carroll, the editor who argued for *Mulligan Stew* knowing it had been turned down by every major house in town, says his reasons were "entirely emotional and intellectual. A rational view would have been that the book was impossible."

It Calms Them Down

Rosset's impulses haven't really changed very much. He disagrees with feminists advocating censorship of hard-core pornography in Times Square. "The idea is that people see bad sex in books and run out and do it," he says. "I don't think that's true—I think it calms them down. But even if it were true, I'd still say you can't interfere. It's part of the risk you have to take."

The impulses at Grove are still pretty much the same, too, according to John Rechy. His new novel, *Rushes*, is scheduled for publication this fall. After publishing one of his books with a larger house, Rechy says he returned to Grove "because they really handle a book as if they love it. More than anything else, that sets them apart."

Just the other day, Rosset received an order from the Francis W. Parker School for plays by Pinter, Ionesco and Stoppard. Rosset marvels at how unthinkable it was 20 years ago that these plays would filter down to the high school level.

It is probably true that a new generation needs a new sensibility, but Rosset thinks Grove can survive—and regenerate. He suspects that a few corporations now regret owning publishing houses.

"Books still are not all that profitable," he says. "That's the safety valve built into it all. You're saved by your own weakness."

— **Randy Sue Coburn**

Alan Swallow

Swallow Press

Alan Swallow

Every story of devotion and integrity begins with a story of love and gratitude. Alan Swallow was born on an irrigated farm in northwestern Wyoming. He was an omnivorous reader. As in many lives not too rich in incidents, books became a form of travel, knowledge, expansion, adventure and enrichment. So at the base of the admirable harmony of his life lies the love of books, a recognition of their value. He worked at a filling station and in between customers he read Haldeman-Julius Publications because they were available to his budget.

"I was tremendously attracted by several things that I learned then: first by the effort of Haldeman-Julius to provide good literature at inexpensive prices—and I suppose that there was planted a small seed of the idea of publishing at some time; second through Haldeman-Julius' publications of magazines and through reading other materials, I became aware of the group we call 'The Little Magazines.' I was certainly impressed with the idealism and the effort of these magazines to put out a quality work without consideration for commercial results."

Many young men have started such idealistic schemes, and many printing presses were inaugurated, but very few were carried into maturity and full expansion as Alan Swallow, Publisher. He had more courage, more persistence and more dedication.

In 1939 he borrowed a hundred dollars from his father and secured a second-hand five-by-eight Kelsey handpress. This was set up in the garage of the apartment where he lived.

This was the beginning.

This was the outline of his activity. What I could read of his character from our long correspondence and only one meeting was the enthusiasms which sustained and recharged him, his delight in his victories, his obstinacy in struggling against the established ways of publication which would seem unconquerable by an individual. The solidity and intelligence in his activity were derived not only from his individual conviction, integrity and obstinacy; it came from his love of writing and his wisdom about writing. He knew that it was his attitude and his construction in publishing which alone would keep quality writing alive. He knew that commercial publishing was the worst enemy of the writer and that this could not be obscured by the example of a few writers materially enriched who so often were quickly emasculated and sterilized by the system, and ceased to be writers altogether.

Perhaps because he was a man from the West, born close to the earth, because he was brought up on the solidity of certain eternal values, he knew the simple truths which commerce so often overlooks. Commerce never concerns itself with seedling, crops, growth, but only with the finished object to be sold. It never concerns itself with the possible dangers of writers dying out, writing dying out. Commerce does not bother with research, experiment, the need for renewal, the protection for writing which may not yield immediate gain. A writer takes too long to grow! Alan Swallow was an educator, among other things, and this may have given him his sense of the future. This is a very important feature in the history of his achievements. He knew that writers needed to be free of exorbitant economic pressure and demand put upon them by commercial publishers, the gruesome test of quick sales, immediate acceptance, of the figures added like figures on a Wall Street ticker tape.

An image comes to my mind when I seek a parallel to his activities. The woodcutting companies buy land, cut down all the trees, and pass on to buy another sector of the forest, leaving the one they decimated like an ugly empty cemetery. The Forest Service, led by another idealist, Gifford Pinchot, came along to replant the devastated land (a devastation which caused floods and droughts) and to teach selective cutting of the mature trees and not the young ones, so as to give the young ones time to grow. The forests were saved from ugly gashes, destroyed land, and so was the future of the trees themselves.

Alan Swallow applied this earthy principle to his publishing. Possibly because he was himself a poet, he also knew that poetry was the fecundating seed of all writing. He was an idealist but not a romantic. The source of his contentment, his philosophical equilibrium and energy, was his wisdom, his pride in growth. He enjoyed the challenge of the difficulties. At one time individual effort was highly regarded in America. Then for a time it was denigrated. Now it has been recognized once more by the direct success of underground films, underground presses, underground theatre; and the Giant Industries were revealed as empty factories while the underground fed its depleted coffers. So once more, individual effort is restored to its proper place; it is the research department of all achievements, for future enrichment of all.

I never saw Alan Swallow waste a moment of anger at commercial publishers. He simply thought they were mistaken in their own self-interest. Shortsighted. He was more intent on creating his own structure which would embody his earthy wisdom. He was a man capable of devotion, selflessness, integrity, but he was practical. His solutions were effective. He proved a man could support his family and yet create a publishing house of impressive achievements. The commercial publishers were ultimately destroying the very source of their wealth. Writers succumbed first of all to a false dream of wealth which only a few would attain, then to a hothouse forcing of their talents, then to a star system which continued to publish the most mediocre work of any writer who had attained a reputation. This meant that the system was destructive to the life of writing itself. Good writers were caught in an absurd race for quick sales, false publicity, and if they failed to pass the first harsh test of economic exigencies they were considered failures. Some of these writers came to Alan Swallow. He made minimal demands on them. He was patient with them. They continued to expand and develop and several among them were recognized as valuable by Big Business later.

His *An Editor's Essays of Two Decades* reveals a quiet sense of basic values, a classical critical faculty, and a devotion to this very regional, native, folkloric literature which has always been at the roots of all national literature. This essentially American literature which the merchandising East wanted so much to produce was actually fed and sustained not by them but by such underground, independent methods. Small magazines, small publishers, private ventures, young presses, kept writing alive even though some of them did not survive.

The only discouragement I ever saw in Alan Swallow was due to his physical handicaps: his heart attack and his leg injury. He could not reduce his activity because it was an expression of his entire personality.

Some people feel that the great burden of an individual achievement killed him. I am not certain about this. When a man has such a need of working at something he believes in, in harmony with his ideas, temperament and convictions, any other form of life would have killed him sooner. True, he might have been helped more. One wishes he had lived longer, to enjoy his victories. But he was given time to make a unique synthesis of all his many talents, as a poet, essayist, critic, teacher and editor, and as a man of action who needed a concrete proof of his service to writing.

— Anais Nin

Noel Young

Capra Press

Capra: Santa Barbara's Big Little Press

An exploding car and a hot tub helped to give Santa Barbara one of the country's most vigorous small publishing companies.

The car was an old La Salle, and back in 1947 an aspiring young poet named Noel Young was in its driver's seat, heading for Monterey. The journey ended, however, in Santa Barbara, where the La Salle blew up.

Deciding to stay here, Young apprenticed himself to a printer and about a year later he installed his own hand-operated printing press in his garage. He originally planned to print up his own poetry and peddle it door-to-door, as Walt Whitman once did. But the skill and care he put into his early "bread and butter" printing—menus, theatre programs, small editions of poetry, etc.—won him increasing recognition as a fine printer. His reputation in that field grew steadily over the years.

About three years ago, the hot tub provided inspiration for a book whose success was the final impetus that moved Young from the craft of printing into that of publishing.

Mainly just for the enjoyment of doing it, he wrote and published a little book on the building and maintenance of hot tubs. (An article in the *Los Angeles Times* recently called the book the "bible" of hot tub enthusiasts around the country.)

Appropriately entitled *Hot Tubs*, the book sold-out two editions of 15,000 copies each and was then sold to Random House. (Young wrote the book under the pen-name Leon Elder, a whimsical backward-rendering of his real name.)

Hot Tubs wasn't the first book Young had published. He had launched the Capricorn Press—later renamed the Capra Press—in 1969, but his printing business was still his main livelihood. That situation changed about three years ago, as we found out when we went to Capra's offices on State Street to talk with Young and sales manager Robert Sheldon, who joined the Capra Press about a year ago.

Interviewer: Did you expect *Hot Tubs* to have the success it did?

Young: *Hot Tubs* was done on a shoestring, when I was still making my living from my printing business. I didn't expect it to be more than a kind of local curiosity. I just had a lot of fun doing it. Then it got big all by itself. I was knocked out—people all over the country were sending orders for the book.

Interviewer: After having established yourself as a printer, was it difficult for you to change course and go into publishing?

Young: Well, it was never a clear-cut decision, like now I'm leaving printing and going into publishing. It was more like an evolution—I had already done nearly thirty books when I was still in the printing business.

After the hot tubs book, I guess that was the time when I decided to turn all of my attention to writing, editing and publishing. So when I went "officially" into being a publisher, I already had those thirty titles to go with, and that helped us get distribution.

As you probably know, if you don't have many titles it's tough getting distribution at first. Right now, we've got about 70 or 80 titles in print.

Interviewer: Why didn't you keep the printing business and go on publishing at the same time?

Sheldon: That would be possible, but they're two different businesses. For a publisher, it's just more complication to do your own printing. Very few publishers do that.

Young: Also, my printing equipment was letterpress equipment. That's a process which is suited best to high-quality printing of under a thousand or so copies of a book. It's a beautiful form of printing, but it's a slow process. It's not really suited to large-volume printing. Most of that is done now with high-speed photo-offset equipment.

I sold my printing business for one dollar to Graham Mackintosh and my son Aaron and the rest of the crew in the printing shop. They're still doing beautiful work.

Interviewer: Your books have been praised for their physical appearance. Do you still retain control over this aspect?

Young: We do all the design of our books—our typesetting is done here in town, and when we send the book off to the actual bookmaker, it's on film and ready to go to press. We control the design, shape and size of our books.

Interviewer: How do you go about soliciting manuscripts for publication?

Young: We don't have to go out and solicit material; it comes in at the rate of almost 2,000 a year, in the form of queries or full manuscripts. It requires somebody reading manuscripts every day—that's usually me, in the evenings.

If the topic is something I don't know much about, I pass it on for reading to one of the other people who work with us. But I like the adventure of going through the day's mail and seeing what's come to us.

Interviewer: How is it that you get so much material without soliciting it?

Sheldon: Well, people may see our books in a bookstore and decide to send their manuscripts to us for consideration. Or sometimes an author has made the rounds of the big publishers without success, and then comes to us. That's how we got our *Great Winemakers of California* book. It was rejected by Doubleday or Random House and Robert Benson, its author, brought it to us. August 10 was the publication date, and we've sold 12,000 copies already. We'll have to reprint it soon. It's a very successful book for us.

Interviewer: For a publisher the size of Capra, how many copies does a book have to sell to be successful?

Sheldon: That depends on how many we print of a particular book. Last February, we brought out a book called *The Blue Train*. It's a novella, which is a tough type of book to sell. We printed 2,500 copies and they're all sold. So for that book, 2,500 copies is quite successful.

Young: On the average, the break-even point on a book for us is about 5,000 copies. If you can sell about half to three-fourths of the number you print, you break-even on a book. You never really know for sure how well a book is doing until a year or more after it comes out because bookstores can return books up to a year after they buy them.

There was one book, a couple of years ago, that seemed to be a giant success—bookstores all over the country were taking it and we even reprinted. But then the rate of returned copies on that book wound up being over 60 percent. So suddenly we really had to sit back and lick our wounds on that one.

Interviewer: Among the books you publish, there's quite a variety of styles and subject matter. Is there any particular orientation behind your choices?

Young: Generally speaking, we try to maintain balance between literature and non-fiction. Publishing is done in two seasons a year, and we do about six or eight titles each season. We always try to have a lead literary title and a lead lifestyle or documentary title. Those are our two main strengths. I turn down a lot of books that I think might well be successful, if they don't seem to "fit" me.

We're a very personal press—there are only four of us in the editorial and production staff and we put out books that reflect what interests us, whether it's in fiction, "functional" books or documentaries.

One thing I'd like to get across, because there's been a lot of confusion about it: we are a "Santa Barbara press," in the sense that we're located here, and all things being equal I favor Santa Barbara authors over others. But we're not a publisher of "local" books, as such.

A lot of people come to us with a great "Santa Barbara idea"—like a tour guide of Santa Barbara, or *Santa Barbara at night*, or the history of a local building, or whatever. But such a book wouldn't sell outside of Santa Barbara.

Anyway, you don't really even need a publisher, with a sales and distribution organization, for a book like that. You can arrange to produce it yourself in enough copies to take around to the local bookstores. The point is, that's not the type of book we publish. We're what is called a "small independent trade publisher," and our books

Young

are intended for a world—or at least national—audience.

Interviewer: How would you sum up your philosophy as a publisher?

Young: I want to show that it's still possible to have a sense of personal level, free enterprise, to run a business in terms of what's really important to you, and not have decisions made by a computerized market-analysis or an anonymous committee. That goes for the people I deal with for auxiliary services, too, like typesetting and so forth. I like to deal with people who meet me face to face and work with me personally, rather than through sales-representatives of great big anonymous outfits.

There aren't many independent presses left in the country—even the big names you're probably familiar with, like Scribner's or Knopf or Random House—even those aren't independent anymore. They've long since been swallowed up by things like RCA and other giant business interests. There are just a few left around the country that are still managed, edited and owned by the people who actually do the work.

So, in this world which is so mechanized, I like to keep the human touch as much as possible. There's a sense of freedom in it, along with a lot of responsibility.

Capra Press is now almost as big as we ever want it to get. If we got much bigger, it wouldn't be a personal expression anymore.

— Ernie Tamminga

Contributors

Eric Burns is a graduate of Jesus College, Cambridge, and now lives in London.

Randy Sue Coburn lives in Washington, D.C. Her articles have appeared recently in *Smithsonian*, *Esquire*, *Washington Post Magazine*, and *Regardies*. She worked on the staff of the *Washington Star* for many years.

Stella Dong is on the staff of *Publishers Weekly*.

Donald Hall lives in Danbury, New Hampshire. An influential poet and critic, his recent books are *Kicking the Leaves* (1978), and *The Weather for Poetry* (1981). He also edited *The Oxford Book of American Literary Anecdotes* (1981).

Richard Kostelanetz is an internationally renowned critic, experimentalist, poet, fiction writer, and visual artist. He lives in New York City. His *The End of Intelligent Writing* is a must for anyone interested in the future of publishing and/or literature.

Anais Nin (1903-1977) was born in Paris, and came to the US in 1914. She is perhaps best known for her diaries but also founded her own press and self-published many of her early works. Some of her books are *House of Incest*; *Delta of Venus*; *Cities of the Interior*; *Linotte*.

William Robson lives in Long Beach, California. Aside from *Southern California Lit Scene*, he published *Holy Doors* (1972), an anthology of poetry, prose, and criticism, *Big Boulevard* magazine, and *A Long Line of Joy* (1978), a collection of poetry, commentary, and interviews.

William F. Ryan lives in Arlington, Virginia. His "Nightside" columns are a mainstay of the *Washington Tribune*. His work has appeared in the *D.C. City Paper*, *Washington Book Review*, and *Virginia Country*. Bill is working on a biography of E. Haldeman-Julius, another American publishing maverick.

Ernie Tamminga, to the best of our knowledge, still lives in Santa Barbara, California, and writes for the *Santa Barbara News & Review*.